DIRE STRAITS
A Visual Biography

Laura Shenton

DIRE STRAITS
A Visual Biography

Laura Shenton

WYMER
PUBLISHING
Bedford, England

First published in Great Britain in 2021
by Wymer Publishing
www.wymerpublishing.co.uk
Tel: 01234 326691
Wymer Publishing is a trading name of Wymer (UK) Ltd

This edition 2023
Copyright © Laura Shenton /Wymer Publishing.

ISBN: 978-1-915246-41-7

Edited by Jerry Bloom.

The Author hereby asserts her rights to be identified
as the author of this work in accordance with sections
77 to 78 of the Copyright, Designs & Patents Act 1988.

All rights reserved. No part of this publication may be
reproduced or transmitted in any form or by any means,
electronic or mechanical, including photocopying, or any
information storage and retrieval system, without written
permission from the publisher.

This publication is sold subject to the condition that it shall not,
by way of trade or otherwise, be lent, re-sold, hired out or
otherwise circulated without the publishers prior consent in any
form of binding or cover other than that in which it is published
and without a similar condition including this condition
being imposed on the subsequent purchaser.

Every effort has been made to trace the copyright holders of the
photographs in this book but some were unreachable. We would
be grateful if the photographers concerned would contact us.

Typeset and Design by Andy Bishop / Tusseheia Creative
Printed by Halstan.

A catalogue record for this book is available from the British Library.

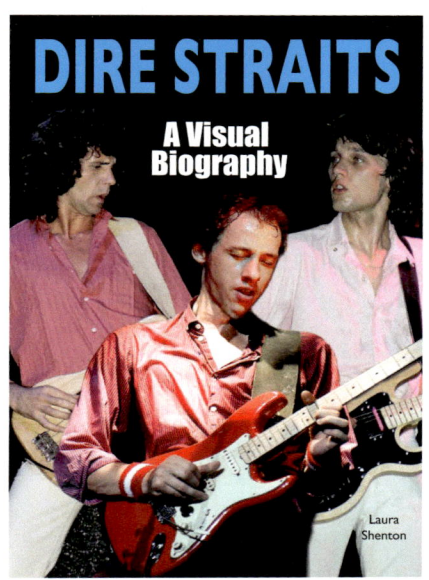

Contents

Preface   11

Chapter One: Sultans Of Swing   13

Chapter Two: Communiqué   49

Chapter Three: Making Movies   89

Chapter Four: Love Over Gold   109

Chapter Five: Brothers In Arms   127

Chapter Six: On Every Street   159

  Appendices: 179

    Band Members

    Discography

    Awards

    Tour Dates

"The random nature of the universe is connected to the random nature of songwriting. There doesn't seem to be much of a formula to me. Every song has a life of its own."

Mark Knopfler — October 1982, Melody Maker

Preface

The first of its kind, this book is a celebration of everything that Dire Straits have done throughout their outstanding tenure.

Well-known for their iconic songs — 'Sultans Of Swing' and 'Money For Nothing' — and Mark Knopfler's excellent leadership, even the more casual music fan has heard of Dire Straits. For those with a more intensive interest in the band though, there is so much to say about their albums and the processes that they went through as part of making each one. And that's before taking into account all of the large-scale tours!

Across several line-up changes and many mixed reviews, Dire Straits' sound has always remained distinctive. They were never a band to modify their style to meet the whims of what else was going on with popular music at the time. With a fascinating discography to their name, the extensive documentation of their achievements that follows in this book is certainly warranted. However, the narrative is an objective one and so rather than this book being an exercise in hero worship, there is a balanced approach to look forward to.

As author of this book, I have no affiliation with Dire Straits or with any of their associates. This book is the result of an accumulation of research inspired by a passion for the band's excellent contribution to music; you're going to see lots of quotes from vintage articles in here. Not only will this help to give an accurate portrayal of what was said about Dire Straits and by the band themselves at the time, but also, there will probably come a time where such material will become harder to source and so it is important to archive it all here.

Do check out the details in the appendices. It really goes to show just how much of a hard-working band Dire Straits were. High-level musicianship and excellent songwriting were just the tip of the iceberg when taking into consideration just how demanding the tour schedules were.

From the early days of performing in the Hope & Anchor pub, to playing large stadiums all over the world, what a journey indeed!

Sultans Of Swing

Dire Straits certainly made their mark in music. As one of the world's best-selling artists — with album sales exceeding over 100 million — they were active from 1977 to 1988 and then again from 1991 to 1995. The *Guinness Book Of British Hit Albums* asserts that the band have graced the UK albums chart for a total of over 1,100 weeks. Formed in London in 1977, the original line-up consisted of Mark Knopfler on lead vocals and guitar, his brother David Knopfler on rhythm guitar and backing vocals, John Illsley on bass guitar and backing vocals and David "Pick" Withers on drums. Their first single, 'Sultans Of Swing', is still one of Dire Straits' most memorable songs to date. It was the beginning of a number of successes; the band — across various line-ups — would go on to have hit singles with 'Romeo And Juliet' (1981), 'Private Investigations' (1982), 'Twisting By The Pool' (1983), 'Money For Nothing' (1985) and 'Walk Of Life' (1985). Dire Straits' most commercially successful album is *Brothers In Arms*. Released in 1985, it has sold over thirty million copies and was the first album to sell a million copies in CD format. Not only that, but *Brothers In Arms* is the eighth-best selling album in UK history.

Dire Straits' musical influences are from a range of sources that cover a broad spectrum: blues, rock, country, jazz and folk. In their early days in particular, their sound was often compared to that of J.J. Cale, Bob Dylan and Bruce Springsteen. Considering the time at which Dire Straits rose to fame, their sound stood out in comparison to the punk rock, new wave and disco styles of music that were popular in the charts at the time. Overall, Dire Straits' rock influence was more inspired by pub rock than that which was more popular by the late seventies.

Across several line-up changes over the years, Mark Knopfler and John Illsley remained as the only permanent members of the band across their tenure. It was in 1995 that Dire Straits disbanded for a final time. Thereafter, Mark Knopfler has gone on to have a sparkling career as a solo artist. He has stated several times that he has no wish to participate in a Dire Straits reunion.

Dire Straits' 1985-1986 world tour saw them perform at *Live Aid* in July in 1985. Their final world tour over 1991 and 1992 resulted in the sale of 7.1 million tickets. As well as many other awards, Dire Straits won four Grammys, three Brits (twice for Best British Group) and two MTV Video Music Awards. 2018 saw the band inducted into the Rock And Roll Hall Of Fame.

From Newcastle, brothers Mark and David Knopfler formed Dire Straits with their friends, John Illsley and Pick Withers. By 1977, Pick Withers already had a music career to his name having been a session drummer for Bert Jansch. He had also been a member of the group Spring, who had recorded an eponymous album on RCA in 1971.

Prior to the band coming together, all the other band members had been working in completely different fields. David Knopfler was a social worker and John Illsley had studied sociology at Goldsmiths College.

In 1968, after studying journalism for a year at Harlow Technical College, Mark Knopfler graduated and landed a job as a reporter and music critic at the *Yorkshire Evening Post*, where he stayed for two years.

As an example of his skills as a music critic the young Knopfler was sent along to St George's Hall, Bradford on 7th December 1969 to review a gig by Family, supported by Deep Purple. With the heading 'Great show from Purple and Family' Mark's review, which was followed by an overview of other musical happenings said: *The Family and Deep Purple concert at St. George's Hall, Bradford, on Sunday, really did come up to expectations.*

Deep Purple belted out their usual stupefying act with guitarist Ritchie Blackmore's roasting solos and Jon Lord's magnificent organ work. The group ended with 'Mandrake Root', complete with strobe light, feedback and general disrespect shown to amplification equipment and musical instruments. Quite astonishing nevertheless. Powerhouse.

Family, with their new member "Polly" on vibes, flute and piano, were quite outstanding. Singer Roger Chapman seemed happier than usual — so did everyone else, come to that. Rob Townsend on his distinctive yellow drum kit charged along. A real little powerhouse, and certainly one of pop's finest drummers.

Bass player John Weider proved again that he is an excellent guitarist, and in another lengthy "duologue" with Townsend, showed his skill on violin.

Bradford is really moving away from the old soul image. Also on the waiting list for St George's Hall are Pink Floyd and The Who, who are set to perform Tommy *on February 11 in a concert arranged by Bradford University Student's Union. The Best.*

Leeds' country blues singer and guitarist Steve Phillips is the best of his type in the country — confirmed last week by Blues artist Ian Anderson in a free concert at the Polytechnic in Leeds. Leeds University blues band Death (why not Life for goodness sake?) are in the process of getting a regular event going in The Adelphi, Lower Briggate, Leeds, on Fridays.

For Knopfler, after two years with the *Yorkshire Evening Post*, he pursued an English degree at Leeds University, where he graduated in 1973.

He was quoted in *Rolling Stone* in November 1985; "The last story I ever wrote for the newspaper — on the day that I left — was the death of Jimi Hendrix. I was in the press room at Leeds Town Hall, 'cause I'd been covering the courts all day, when the news editor came in and said, 'Hello, lad, Jimmy Henderson or Jimi Hendrix or whatever the bloody hell he's called died. Did you know him? Well, we haven't got any time. I'm putting you straight onto copy.' I was stunned. I don't recall what I wrote. I said some stuff, left the paper and got drunk."

After graduating he moved to London to pursue his own career in music. A struggling musician, he moved into a room that had no heat and slept on an ambulance stretcher instead of a bed.

In November 1985 Mark told *Rolling Stone*; "When I left university, I went down to London and got in this band called Brewers Droop. I was with them for maybe two months. They were sort of an obscene R&B Cajun outfit. Brewer's droop is something that you suffer from when you've been drinking too much and you can't get it up. They actually had a deal with RCA that was just falling apart when I joined them. But I did a bunch of gigs with them. That was my first taste of playing on the college and big-clubs circuit. I did a little bit of recording with Brewers Droop at Rockfield Studios. I don't think any of it ever came out. After that, I just starved to death, basically. It got pretty tough until I got hold of this teaching job that saved my life."

The job in question was teaching English part-time at Loughton College for a more stable income, and he worked there until 1977.

Nevertheless, his brief time with Brewers Droop gave Mark his first encounter with Pick Withers the band's drummer.

"Then I had a band called the Café Racers," he recalled. "Which was the name of a kind of motorcycle, not a particular make, just a customised street bike. We played around the pubs and the college where I was teaching."

Mark told *Circus* in January 1981; "The Café Racers were doing R&B, rockabilly-type stuff. We played in pubs in London. I just had this thirty-watt amplifier — we used to stick it up on two wooden chairs. I used to play a Gibson Les Paul Special with a pick."

After a divorce and with financial struggles to boot, Mark moved into brother David's flat where John Illsley also lived. The three of them made a decision to form a band and it was upon the recruitment of Pick Withers that they started rehearsing.

They played their first gig at the Crossfields Festival on 26th June 1977 under the name of Café Racers, but soon settled on Dire Straits in direct reference to their financial situation.

Mark was quoted in *Rolling Stone* in January 1983; "The day I finished university, I went to London and joined a band and promptly ended up completely destitute, divorced and selling guitars to stay alive… I only got the teaching thing because I was trying to be a musician and I was starving to death."

He was quoted in *Circus* in January 1981; "I never missed the paper for a second… I have missed bits of teaching, but after the third year of it, I really wanted to play music all the time."

A few months of rehearsals and borrowed money later, Dire Straits had enough behind them to record a demo. Recorded on 24th July 1977 at London's Pathway Studios and consisting of five songs — 'Down To The Waterline', 'Water Of Love', 'Wild Wild West' and 'Sacred Loving', it included the yet-to-be appreciated track, 'Sultans Of Swing'.

Mark Knopfler was quoted in *Guitar World* in October 2008; "'Sultans Of Swing' was originally written on a National Steel guitar in an open tuning, although I never performed it that way. I thought it was dull, but as soon as I bought my first Strat in 1977, the whole thing changed, although the lyrics remained the same. It just came alive as soon as I played it on that '61 Strat — which remained my main guitar for many years and was basically the only thing I played on the first album — and the new chord changes just presented themselves and fell into place. It's really a good example of how the music you make is shaped by what you play it on, and is a lesson for young players. If you feel that you're not getting enough out of a song, change the instrument — go from an acoustic to an electric or vice versa, or try an open tuning. Do something to shake it up. As for the actual solo, it was just more or less what I played every night. It's just a Fender Twin and the Strat, with its three-way selector switch jammed into a middle position. That gives the song its sound, and I think there were quite a few five-way switches installed as a result of that song."

Regarding the writing of 'Sultans Of Swing', an early tape recording of the process — according to John Illsley — had more of a country and western feel to it. Knopfler was quoted in *Rolling Stone* in November 1985; "It had a completely different musical thing to it. I wrote it on an acoustic guitar. Then when I started playing it on the Strat, it came out different, just because I was using a different guitar. I actually saw a jazz band one night in south London. It reminded me that whenever a band plays something like 'Creole Love Call', you realise how beautiful that music is. It's important to listen, to know about that music. It doesn't matter whether it's Ellington or a traditional jazz band or Roland Kirk who plays it. It's fine music."

The beginning of Dire Straits' journey was the result of sheer passion for the music. Knopfler said; "It's amazing what I've done to get into bands — hitchhike up and down the country with a heavy electric guitar, getting on buses with two guitars to go up to an audition. I remember once hitchhiking home up to Newcastle on Christmas Day from the other end of the country, the snow all around, nobody on the roads, with a guitar and a bag, standing in the middle of nowhere. You've really got to want to do it. For me and John, in the early stages of the Dire Straits thing, there was a collective willpower that went into it. If you're a lazy son of a bitch, you're just going to sit around and complain 'cause there's nothing happening. We weren't."

Many years later in May 2019 during an interview for *Record Collector* Knopfler continued to reiterate the same beliefs; "Music was what I wanted to do so badly. That's important. It has to be such a part of you. The desire is nearly everything. That's the thing which will keep you going. You need to have what an American friend of mine calls "the burn". You've got to have the burn! That defines what kind of person you are — falling in love with music, with the guitar, being consumed by it. I still get it when I walk into the rehearsal room and see the gear. That's my ground."

After a performance at London's Rock Garden, Dire Straits took their demo tape to MCA in Soho. It proved not to be fruitful though.

They then took the tape to Charlie Gillett, a DJ with a show on BBC Radio London by the name of *Honky Tonk*. It was hoped that Gillett would be able to give them some advice. Such was Gillett's appreciation of the demo that he began to play 'Sultans Of Swing' on his show (the first time being 31st July 1977).

David Knopfler said in *Record Mirror* in September 1978; "We wanted some advice on our music so we sent the tape to Charlie Gillett. We weren't really expecting airplay but very nicely he put it on the show. We're not out for massive media coverage, we're not out for people to define what we're doing or to pigeonhole us into neat compartments. We want to produce good records for people to have a good time."

Released in 1979, *The Honky Tonk Demos* record features demo tapes by several artists that were first played by Charlie Gillett on his BBC Radio London show between 1975 and 1978. Regarding 'Sultans Of Swing', Gillett wrote for the liner notes: "This was one of those extra special songs that seemed to grow richer with every play, as different guitar licks made their point and the narrative of the song became clear. Without any premonition of the possible repercussions, I slipped the track into the running order for the show on 31st July 1977 following Bonnie Raitt's 'Good Enough' and just ahead of Ry Cooder and Squeeze. It turned out that half the A&R men of London were listening that Sunday, and they rushed to the phone to ask who that tape was by, 'you know, the one that sounded like an American band'. Arnold of Virgin was having a bath, Chris of Chrysalis was driving to a cricket match and lost reception as I was giving the name of the band, Nigel of Ensign was also in his car, and Johnny from Phonogram was having a shower. Richard Williams, editor of *Time Out*, sat spellbound in his own front room. The boys in the band weren't even tuned in, they were helping a friend move house and missed it. So I played the song again the next week, and then worked through the other songs on the tape until Dire Straits joined the Darts and Rico at the *Honky Tonk* Summer Party on 11th September. I remember the sense of responsibility I felt when they said they had given up their previous careers and were going to commit themselves to music

— it seemed like such a big risk, especially with a name like Dire Straits."

Just a couple of months of Gillett playing 'Sultans Of Swing' on the radio saw Dire Straits in possession of a recording contract with Vertigo Records, a division of Phonogram. October 1977 saw Dire Straits record demos of 'In The Gallery', 'Southbound Again' and 'Six Blade Knife' for BBC Radio London. In the November, they recorded demos of 'Setting Me Up', 'Eastbound Train' and 'Real Girl'.

In October 1977, *New Musical Express* reported on a performance that took place at the Hope And Anchor; "Not an obvious little band, this. On the face of it, Dire Straits tread a hack course through easy rocking American vapidity, minus the Californian harmonies and the surface gloss that distinguishes most LA product from everything else, and hence is mundane in the sweaty environs of London town. Or so I thought when I encountered them some months ago. Decidedly unmoved by what seemed like four people trying to sound like J.J. Cale, I promptly forgot the name. But first impressions often bely the truth, and I thank Charlie Gillett for opening my ears. For the past few weeks he's been playing a tape of theirs on *Honky Tonk* radio show that reveals music of quite different proportions, and seeing them a second time proved me wrong and him right. Dire Straits sound just like J.J. Cale, though to my mind that isn't much to boast about (either I'm missing the irony or anyone who writes a song like 'Cocaine' must be a fool). They play relaxed and urbane, not to say laid back, with a roughneck funk laziness that matches Cale for ease and authenticity. Other comparison points are Ry Cooder, occasionally Beefheart, and the blues-gone-sour of Randy Newman's 'Gone Dead Train'. What sets Dire Straits apart is the slide from the commonplace to the sublime. Mark Knopfler, who sings, plays guitar and seems to be the group's prime mover, has a dry and cool voice that at first disguises and then highlights the wry songs. His tone is acerbic, dispassionate, and combined with the band's tasteful restraint, it creates a feel that resembles Lou Reed's *Coney Island Baby*, but mercifully without the limp-wrist and wasted contrivance. Mentioning Lou Reed though, inevitability leads to the wrong conclusions. There are no New York echoes in Dire Straits apart from an occasional tendency towards wordy Springsteen-like romance. Rather the four piece line-up (drums, bass and two guitars) work an unusual combination of backporch funk and wry, sophisticated songcrafting that demands almost a category of its own. Although their musical territory isn't novel, they play with a consummate grasp of the essential qualities of the style that makes up for any musicianly shortcomings. As with the music, a casual listen could miss the inherent strength, and it may take some tuning in to pick up on the considerable subtleties Dire Straits possess, but the effort is well worth the reward. They encored with a walking version of Chuck Berry's 'Nadine', arranged in a way The Band would have been proud of, and proved themselves to be not merely hot, but sultry."

Regarding Dire Straits' early gigs, it was considered by one journalist (Steve Clark) in *New Musical Express* in January 1978; "The band are predominantly low key and didn't live up to my expectations when I saw them live for the first (and only) time. NME's Paul Rambali also drew a blank on his first exposure — but the second time he found them quite enthralling. This I'm willing to believe, since Mark's songs are certainly tuneful and, as far as I'm concerned, perfectly relevant."

Clark reported in the same feature; "In the metropolis, Charlie Gillett's Radio London show, *Honky Tonk*, is renowned in commitment to music with broad-based minority appeal. He'll play something by an obscure Cajun accordionist, yet won't ignore more popular artists like Ry Cooder or J.J. Cale, who make music instantly recognisable as their own but owe a lot to various musical traditions. Charlie also played lots of rockabilly — the fifties kind, contemporary interpretations by say, Darts, and lots of R&B and country. It's all, for want of better phrase, genuine music. Anyway, one Sunday in the latter half of last year, he played a tape by an unknown South London based band given to him only three days earlier, which would normally be too late for that week's show since he makes up his playlist on Thursdays. Meaning, Charlie must have been impressed. The band was Dire Straits and the tape, recorded under the strictest of budgets in a small Highbury studio, created quite a stir. Rock critic and current *Time Out* editor Richard Williams was so impressed that he contacted the band and offered to cash-in his life insurance to finance a production deal. Such dramatic measures weren't called for. The cut, 'Sultans Of Swing', didn't go unheard by several record company people, who promptly got off their butts to check things out. Despite not so much as a single bow to the seemingly omnipresent new wave, Dire Straits were, according to Strait-person Mark Knopfler, inundated with record company attention. After the airplay the phone barely stopped ringing at the Deptford council flat where the band rehearsed, and as battered ole '77 drew to a close the Straits signed a "major deal" with Phonogram."

In the same feature, the journalist revealed that in a conversion over lunch at Eytie Eaterie, Mark Knopfler and John Illsley were reluctant to give too much information away but did reveal that they had signed a six-figure deal worth more than £100,000.

In January 1978, the members of Dire Straits were introduced in *New Musical Express* as follows: "Straits are Mark Knopfler (guitar, vocals, most of the songs), his brother David (rhythm guitar), John Illsley (bass), Pick Withers (drums). Pick, who has played with the likes of Bert Jansch and Michael Chapman, is the only one with any professional music pedigree to speak of, though the Knopfler brothers have played together on an informal basis since their teens. At twenty-eight, Mark is the heart of Dire Straits. He formed the group last summer as a vehicle for the songs he had been piling up, having previously managed to combine playing in a low-profile London pub band, Café Racers, and teaching English at Loughton Tech in Essex… Café Racers concentrated on rockabilly, Everly Brothers material, and R&B. Knopfler's contribution was just to play guitar, utilising the kind of hard-hitting Wilko Johnson/Mick Green licks that don't get aired during a Dire Straits set… The first thing you notice about Dire Straits is Knopfler's guitar playing. He uses an ancient Fender Strat and amp to create what may well be a unique tone, very brittle and well-defined. You can spot shades of J.J. Cale, Clapton, Hank B. Marvin, fifties alumni like James Burton, and even Django Reinhardt, as well as the aforementioned rockabilly influences in his playing." Knopfler was quoted; "Collectively the band can lay its hands on a tradition of stuff that it can bring to bear on what we're doing now."

David Knopfler was quoted in *Melody Maker* in March 1978; "Suppose we were writers for another band and we had to do something that was on a totally different wavelength to anything else that we've done. It would still come out with all sorts of guitar licks that Mark would inevitably bring to bear on it and still people would say that it's got something from somewhere else on it… I think we're very conscious that other people are going to impose images upon us as opposed to being conscious of images within ourselves. Especially in Britain, where you get the feeling that the music press have identified something within a matter of minutes of it being public, and a week later the mystery has been plucked out of it so they say 'well thank you and good night.' But if you started worrying about it, you'd be doing somersaults all over the place."

To which brother Mark added; "If you're confident of the substance, that should in itself be — if you like — an image. What we try to do is preserve a certain vibe. Get across a certain spirit, and the spirit is the most important thing. Albums to come will perhaps be musically more innovative without really dealing in the area of advanced R&B, if you like. I'm interested in what everybody's doing, in life, and I just hope to reflect that all the time."

In January 1978, *Record Mirror* reported on a performance that took place at London's Rock Garden; "The support band at the Rock Garden sweatshop were new wavers Cheap Stars. One of their songs, all of which lasted a statutory two minutes, was called

'It's Obvious'. I'm sorry to say this summed up their music for me. But Dire Straits were a different proposition. With a name like that I was half-expecting yet another new wave band with some phoney axe to grind about frustrated youth, but no. They turned out to be a funky little four-piece combo whose main musical objective is to make people dance. This they certainly did. For anyone with the music in them it's impossible to keep still while you watch them — you've got to tap your feet at the very least. If you try to imagine a J.J. Cale-type voice combined with an intensified version of the rhythm and general feeling of Eric Clapton's 'Lay Down Sally' single, then you have an idea of what Dire Straits are about. In fact the intro of their first number, 'Southbound Again', could have been old Slow Hand himself as its infectious beat was helped along by a couple of rhythm guitars and a bass. There were more where that came from — 'Six Blade Knife', 'Eastbound Train', 'Down To The Waterline', 'In The Gallery', 'Real Girl' — all played with some *real* musicianship and not a little flair. They're regular visitors to the Rock Garden and deserve to be seen, and to make some progress. But like I said, it's not music to keep still to."

Journalist Tony Stewart reported in April 1978 on a performance that took place at London's Marquee; "One explanation for Dire Straits' metropolitan popularity is that after a vigorous duffing by new wave aggression over the last eighteen months, London gig-goers are now looking for entertainment without intimidation. The band offer that, quietly working through their set at the Marquee almost unaware of the audience's presence. Their act's devoid of histrionics, but still possesses an awesome mood. Because of this, it'd be wrong to explain away their success as merely a tame alternative. Not only are they excellent musicians schooled in blues, J.J. Cale, Dylan and Reed, but guitarist-singer Mark Knopfler, the most brilliant of the four, also exudes an aura of malevolence. It's there in his stance, with the concentrated moodiness of his intricate playing, and his dark, sonorous vocals. The lyrics, particularly of 'Six Blade Knife', are stretched like a taut cord through the song, and the only sign of fraying comes with Knopfler's own cutting guitar lines. But the tension's never relaxed. Much of their style, especially the superb integration of David Knopfler's rhythm guitar, the wide bass tracks from John Illsley, and Pick Withers' sharp, percussive economy with Mark's musical control, is inspired by Cale. But they use it as a grounding, and a scope of their material is broader than J.J.'s. Their main concern is the evocation of moods — sometimes unfortunately so when a wad of similar styles appears in the set, and the arrangements are distinctive enough to provide the necessary contrast. For instance, 'Setting Me Up' is placed between 'Real Girl' and 'Sultans Of Swing', presumably because it's taken at the same brisk pace. But the song doesn't make it, with a thick line drawn between Mark Knopfler and the rhythm section. Elsewhere their approach works. 'Eastbound Train' is an inventive reminder of the forties swing era given a contemporary flavour. And the effect bears some comparison to Tom Waits' writing technique on *Foreign Affairs*. Criticisms are to be expected with any band not yet a year old, who've only just recorded their debut album. Most significantly there are moments of gloomy introspection, hardly helped by their apparent hesitance even to nod to the crowd between numbers. Nonetheless all their excellent qualities are frequently aired, as musicians and songwriters, and the closer, 'Sultans Of Swing' is their definitive song. On that you can't help but consider how inappropriate an adjective as *dire* is in their name."

Whilst many were keen to liken Dire Straits' sound to J.J. Cale, Ry Cooder and Bob Dylan, Mark Knopfler keenly credited a broader range of musical influences regarding what had inspired him. "Musically I've always been interested in everything," he told *New Musical Express* in January 1978. "At the same time I was getting off on the Stones, I'd be playing with people picking out 'The Dallas Rag' on steel guitar."

Speaking to *Rolling Stone* in November 1985 he expanded with; "A lot of dead ones: Robert Johnson, Lonnie Johnson. B.B. King, who's very much alive, is a big influence. I heard *Live At The Regal* when I was sixteen, and that was a great moment, 'cause I felt that a triangle was formed on that record: guitar, voice and audience, and it was amazing to hear. There's also the fact that on his records the guitar seems to do some of the work of the singer — his guitar has such a clear voice. Maybe that appeals to me because I'm not much of a singer in the conventional sense, certainly not like B.B. King is. So my guitar becomes another, better voice I can use. When I was a little kid, I sang Everly Brothers songs with a friend of mine. I really tried to sing well, and I think we did, for kids. But in general, I think singers absorb the influence of other singers. Eric Clapton's one of my favourite singers. People don't give him enough credit for his singing. As a singer, he's the white Ray Charles. Bob Dylan's another influence on my singing. I don't hear it as much as other people seem to, but I know he's in there, in my phrasing. A lot of my favourite singers, people like Tom Waits, Ry Cooder, J.J. Cale, they're not technically great. But to me, that's what makes them special."

And again in 1978 in *Record Mirror* on his vocal comparisons, Mark said; "My voice may have been likened to Dylan, but I'm not out to copy anybody — it's just a certain growl I have."

****

Dire Straits' first album was recorded at Notting Hill's Basing Street Studios in February 1978. Rhett Davies engineered on it. It was produced by Muff Winwood, brother of Steve. Winwood had, like his brother, been a member of the Spencer Davis Group in the sixties before taking up a role in A & R for Island Records. By the early seventies he had already produced records for the likes of Sutherland Brothers & Quiver, Sparks, Mott The Hoople and former Argent frontman Russ Ballard.

Dire Straits' eponymous album was first released in the UK on Vertigo Records. Originally formed in 1970, Vertigo initially focussed on the heavier side of rock with the likes of Black Sabbath, Uriah Heep, Warhorse, and later Status Quo and Thin Lizzy. By 1976 they were also signing notable new acts such as Graham Parker and the short-lived Bethnal. Whilst Dire Straits' music sat comfortably alongside these other acts, they would soon outstrip them all with regards to popularity.

In the States Vertigo's new signing soon came to the attention of Karin Berg, an A&R representative at Warner Bros. in New York. She felt that Dire Straits' music was something that would do well with a US audience but upon taking the proposal to the rest of the team, only one other person agreed with her at first.

Many of the songs on the debut album are reflective of Mark Knopfler's experiences in Newcastle, Leeds and London. Images of Newcastle are recalled in 'Down To The Waterline' and 'In The Gallery' pays tribute to Leeds artist Harry Phillips. 'Wild West End' and 'Lions' were inspired by Mark Knopfler's early experiences in London.

One day in 1977, Mark Knopfler and John Illsley went to an art gallery in London's West End that was being run by a friend of theirs. It was during the ride home to their apartment in South London that Mark sat in the back seat of the car writing at lightning-fast speed. Illsley was quoted in *Rolling Stone* in November 1985; "We just couldn't believe the stuff that was in this gallery — bits of string, bricks piled up in a corner, garbage cans strewn all over the floor. We got to the flat, and he stayed writing in the back seat. So I went upstairs and made myself a cup of tea. Thirty minutes later, he finally came in. 'I just finished this song,' he said. And that was 'In the Gallery'. He wrote the whole thing between Shaftesbury Avenue and Deptford."

Mark told *The New York Times* in November 1980; "I was a cub reporter when I was around twenty, and in a lot of my songs I'm just reporting what I see." Two years earlier he said, "I find the atmosphere in cities tremendously stimulating. Maybe you could call some of the songs city electric blues."

On writing songs that were of relevance, Mark explained in 1978; "It ain't my thing to be talking about going down the road to Mexico. It's got bog-all to do with me. I'm in a constantly-discovering situation, but when it comes to songwriting I'm sticking to what I know about. Our album will be something to put on when you come home from the pub."

When asked his opinion on the present state of music in 1978, he told *Melody Maker*; "It's the same as anything else. As buildings or photographs. Most songs don't deliver the goods, as far as I'm concerned. Most music sucks. Most music is awful. Maybe rubbish is the wrong word to use, because for whatever purpose it's being produced, it's all right. But in terms of music that is supposed to be meaningful, there is too much which says 'I am oh-so sensitive', or the opposite for that matter."

John Illsley added; "Essentially, music is very reflective of what a society's actually about. In a sense, punk music is not relevant on one level to us, but on another it is. It's very hard to say whether you hate it or love it."

Even later on in Dire Straits' tenure, in response to the question of which of their songs are completely written from his own perspective and experiences, Mark Knopfler told *Musician* in September 1985; "I suppose 'Hand In Hand' and 'Water Of Love' because I was so fed up. I felt I was going no place. I could see my future stretching out in front of me long and bleak."

Whilst Dire Straits' lyrics were observational, they weren't done with the intention to persuade anyone of a particular viewpoint. "Being a guitarist doesn't give me the right to voice my opinions on music on the world," said Mark in 1978. "Maybe some people have over-inflated ideas about themselves. They assume that if they appeal to a large section of the public then they have the right to shoot their mouths off. All I want to do at the moment is produce good music. We're trying to get across a certain spirit."

"A guy who owns a record store in Stockton" was quoted in *Sounds* in July 1978; "Dire Straits are a British band who sing about England, that's what I like about them. So many bands get off on the USA." To which the journalist considered; "He couldn't have said it better. No hype, no image building, just get up and go. Throughout the three gigs I saw, the audience seemed to constantly rise to the occasion when 'Lions' came up, which is kind of British."

Of the intent behind the first album, Mark said in *Melody Maker* in March 1978; "Partly it will be getting rid of that history I talked of. In a way it goes from Newcastle to Leeds to London, from side one right the way to the end. It's not exactly a diary, because musically we're always discovering, but I hope the songs are vaguely in a sequence that is related to reality, to what actually happened. I hope it doesn't sound inflated, but I do think the songs smack of something more universally than just my own little world. That's why I hesitate to call it a diary. 'Sultans Of Swing', I hope, works on a number of different perspectives."

For the recording of their first album, Mark Knopfler used several guitars of which included a pair of red Fender Stratocasters — a 1961 and a 1962 model. On 'Water Of Love' and 'Wild West End', he played his 1938 National Style O 14 fret guitar (this legendary guitar went on to be used for the *Brothers In Arms* cover artwork — Knopfler bought it in the early seventies from Steve Phillips. The guitar has featured on all Dire Straits' albums and all Mark Knopfler solo albums since). On 'Setting Me Up', Mark Knopfler played a black Telecaster Thinline. Also on the debut album, David Knopfler played a black Fender Stratocaster and a Harmony Sovereign acoustic guitar.

The debut album reached number two in the US (released on Warner Bros. in October) and to number five in the UK (released on Vertigo in June). It was later certified double platinum in both countries. It also hit the top of the album charts in Germany, Australia and France. It was released on Mercury Records in Canada. Impressively, the debut album spent a total of one hundred and thirty-two weeks on the UK albums chart.

'Sultans Of Swing' got to number four in the US in the early spring of 1979, thus becoming a hit five months after the release of the album there. It was thereafter that 'Sultans Of Swing' caught on in the UK charts where it got to number eight. *New York Rocker* reviewed the single in February 1979; "Just out this month as an American single (and possible hit), but out in June last year in England, this quasi-Dylanesque tribute to trad bands has a haunting tune and the crispest, most tasteful guitar work heard in many years."

It would certainly be misplaced to think of Dire Straits as an overnight success though. Mark Knopfler was quoted in *Guitarist* in December 2018; "It was probably fast by a lot of other people's standards, but I felt as though I had been working all my life towards it. I was twenty-eight when 'Sultans Of Swing' broke, when that first album burst open all round the world. We were still living in Deptford, and with the record deals back then when you first signed, they wouldn't give you any money for eighteen months. I think they're still like that today, actually. So it was number one all over the world, but I didn't get any money from it for ages, and we were still living there for a good while. But I managed to move up the road after a few years. All those deals get renegotiated, in return for which you give them more albums, that's how it works. And it slowly edges up to where you get a reasonable royalty."

A sense of maturity by the time they hit commercial success is probably something that would go in the band's favour throughout their tenure. Mark Knopfler certainly saw it that way; "Touring is tough. If we'd been eighteen when the first album started going nuts all over the world we'd probably be lucky to be alive right now. I think it's only the fact that we had some semblance of sanity early on that we managed to get through it more or less intact."

In some countries, 'Water Of Love' was also released as a single. It got to number fifty-four in Australia and to number twenty-eight in the Netherlands. In November 1988, the 'Sultans Of Swing' single was re-released in the UK in order to promote Dire Straits' greatest hits compilation, *Money For Nothing*, which was released in the October of that year. *Dire Straits* was remastered and reissued along with the rest of the band's catalogue for a 1996 release. It wasn't until 2000 that those albums saw a US release though.

On the original album release, there was a slightly shorter version of 'Sultans Of Swing' withy the last few seconds of the guitar solo at the end of the song omitted. The full-length version is included on the remastered edition of the album. Cassette releases of the original album often have the tracks from side one of the LP on side B and the tracks for side two of the LP on side A. On the French release, 'Wild West End' is interchanged with 'Down To The Waterline' in order to make the running time of each side of the tape more balanced. The cover art was designed by Hothouse — they commissioned the painting from Chuck Loyola.

The album was reviewed in *New Musical Express* in June 1978; "Dire Straits are the only non-new wave act on the London pub circuit to have received consistently good reviews these past few months. Fronted by maverick guitarist/songwriter/vocalist Mark Knopfler, Straits' music is largely inspired by the American south — J.J. Cale and countless rockabilly performers. But unlike many of his predecessors, Knopfler isn't afraid to sing about his own lifestyle. He doesn't invent experiences, or sing about places he's only ever heard of through listening to Chuck Berry records."

"Typically, Straits' best-known song, 'Sultans Of Swing', is not a paean to a jazz group jamming on a New Orleans pavement. Rather, it's a song about a bunch of "amateurs" strutting their stuff in a South London pub in which Knopfler sings of the local kids, weaned on Rod Stewart, who 'don't give a damn about any trumpet playing band.' 'Wild West End' is Knopfler's evocation of London street life. It's not the same view that, say, Jimmy Pursey has of the street of London, but it's just as real — and err, relevant. Unfortunately, Dire Straits' debut doesn't live up to my admittedly great expectations."

"In fact, with the sole exception of 'Six Blade Knife', side one is pretty much a washout. Even the quality of Knopfler's material and playing can't disguise the rest of the band's seemingly indifferent performance and Muff Winwood's unsympathetic production. Winwood's production — bright and trebly — is too tasteful by half."

"Dire Straits' music is about getting your hands dirty. This album is squeaky clean. The backup musicians are mixed too far back. Often the drumming sounds humanoid, the bass unimaginative, the rhythm guitar non-existent. I'm not asking for a host of harps and the London Symphony Orchestra Choir, but a little more arranging would have improved things no end. Certainly, the Straits' music is about restraint, but too much white space in on show here."

"Still, side two makes it by dint of Knopfler's excellent songs and playing. 'Sultans Of Swing' opens the side in impressive style sounding a lot like Clapton covering J.J. Cale ought to sound (incidentally, if Clapton's short on material for his new album, a skim through the gems on sale here should save the day). Straits are deceptively tight as they trip confidently through the changes, Knopfler's vocal phrasing a dead ringer for Dylan's and his guitar choruses, Stratocaster-sharp, not unlike post-Cream Clapton — though with more space between the notes. The following 'In The Gallery' is just as good with its reggae flavour. Knopfler's solo is a rare treat. It starts out taut and pithy, yet seconds later is beautifully lyrical. 'Wild West End' echoes John Martyn and has a strong hook, while the closing 'Lions' is marked by a nicely resolved set of changes."

"Nevertheless, my overriding impression is of potential only half-fulfilled, and of a great deal of talent squandered. Hopefully, Dire Straits will be capable of exercising more collective clout by the time of their second album and won't once again select a producer whose incapable of maximising their ability."

(As it just so happens, different producers would be used for their next album; Jerry Wexler and (credited as B. Bear) Barry Beckett).

Sounds also reviewed the album in the same month; "Charlie Gillett, he of impeccable taste on the BBC Radio London *Honky Tonk* programme, has been raving about this outfit for some time now, but for once I honestly can't see what the fuss is about. A quick census of opinion around the office reveals that 'they're not bad live' and 'the single's good'. Having lived with the album for a weekend, I'm not so sure. Sure, I agree with the sentiments of Northern lads singing the blues about life in London, but drawing inspiration from such situations obviously has its limitations as soon becomes apparent through songs like 'Southbound Again', pangs of grief about crossing the Tyne, or in-town observations of 'Wild West End' delivered at a crawl-along pace that makes the area sound even less wild than it is. Most of the songs are played at the same mid-pace, which drags after a time and it is the lack of variety in momentum that really holds the band back. They seem to be content with building up neat country-rock rhythms and sticking there. Their writer Mark Knopfler tackles the somewhat monotonous vocals and just occasionally adds a spicy riff or lick that builds your hopes up but rarely amounts to much more. No, I'm sorry, Deptford sound or not, I think I'll sit this one out."

The *Reading Evening Post* considered more positively in July 1978; "A supreme album from an amazing new band, who seem to have emerged from nowhere, and must now rank as London's hottest property bar none. The real strength of these nine immaculate songs lies in Mark Knopfler's expert guitar playing. Influenced by J.J. Cale, Eric Clapton and Ry Cooder, Knopfler tunes sound so American, it's difficult to think of Dire Straits as an English band. It's hard to pick out highlights here — every track is a real joy — but 'In The Gallery' and 'Wild West End' stand out for their splendid structure, rhythm and lyrics, as well as Knopfler's almost uncanny sympathy for Pick Withers' drumming. As fine a rock recording as you're likely to hear in '78."

The comment about Knopfler's performance sounding in sympathy with Pick Withers'

drumming is spot on in terms of, the first album has very much a "live" quality about it — that is to say that the band sound very much together and aware of what each other are doing on each track. It really comes across that what each band member does is a complement to what the others are doing.

From *North Wales Weekly News* in July 1978: "An authoritative debut album from a four-man band who have been impressing London audiences in the past few months. It's the style and tone of the guitar-playing that takes this LP out of the ordinary, sounding similar to the latter work of Eric Clapton or J.J. Cale. But its biggest flaw is that every song tends to lean towards the same style. Still, it stands out from the bunch, notably the opening track, 'Down To The Waterline', and 'Sultans Of Swing'. Catch a listen."

The *Hammersmith & Shepherds Bush Gazette* considered in August 1978; "The material may show a wide selection of styles, but all are easy on the ear and ultimately satisfying — even if the influences of the mighty Bob Dylan and Lou Reed are a little too obvious here and there. Highspot for me is 'Water Of Love', a slow, rolling song with a definite hypnotic effect."

Melody Maker reviewed *Dire Straits* in June 1978; "For a moment back there I was worried. Dire Straits, the finest new band to hit London's club trail last year, made a disappointing start to their recording career with 'Eastbound Train' on the *Front Row Festival* compilation. True, circumstances weren't ideal, but the question had to be posed: would the Dire Straits ever be able to get the subtlety and seductiveness of their music across on record? The answer, thank God, is a resounding yes — in this debut album, producer Muff Winwood has captured them at their very best."

"For a band in existence for less than a year it's a supreme achievement. It bears no comparison with the 'Eastbound Train' Straits, though there were a mere couple of months between the two recordings. What shines through the album is the maturity of the music. The band has completely ignored all the usual attention-getters of the young and raw — the gratuitous solos, the metallic riffs, the grinding simplicity and repetition. The Straits deal in moods and shadings. Their superb songs never rush into false climaxes, but cruise smoothly along, mostly at mid-tempo, on deep, rich melodies."

"Mark Knopfler, the band's amazingly talented lead guitarist (and singer, and writer) never resorts to the crass, but picks at melody, sometimes delicately, sometimes aggressively, until he has extracted the juice. The effect of this is to win over the listener by deception (in the best way possible) rather than battering him/her into submission — once you've got the hang of the melody, you sit back and enjoy it. Every single note of Mark's guitar (or so it seems) can be savoured at leisure, every slight change in vocal expression takes on significance."

"This, of course, is more the sort of music we usually associate with American bands. With Dire Straits there can be no confusion. Their lyrics are distinctively British, none more so than the joyful love affair with the more seedy area of central London. 'Wild West End' — sharpness of observation and an ability to express it in intelligent and comprehensible language are two important assets of the writing. The songs are full of examples. But far and away the most important aspect of the writing is the way it's matched with music and performance. Any of the album's songs would do as an example, so three favourites. 'Six Blade Knife' is thick with menace, lead guitar cutting and stabbing (appropriately enough) into the gorgeous rhythm, voice alternately slurring and snarling the lyrics. A sinister, eerie, almost frightening number this. 'Sultans Of Swing' has, for some bizarre reason best known to Phonogram executives, been re-cut as a single. It's difficult to imagine a better version than this bittersweet one, with its acutely observed lyrics about a trad band playing in South London. Unlike 'Guitar George', who's strictly rhythm, 'he doesn't want to make it cry and sing', Mark does just that in two magnificent solos. 'In The Gallery' is the band's most aggressive performance. Lead guitar is in vicious form, biting and scratching at the jerky reggae rhythm, while vituperative vocals lay into an art establishment that lauds the untalented while ignoring the gifted."

The review continued: "No mention so far of the rest of the band — an occupational hazard when you're led by such a multi-talented musician. Yet their role is crucial to the success of the album — not one of the songs would be worth a damn without their imaginative work on the nuts and bolts of the music. The Straits deal in subtle textures — they are the indispensable weavers. So, ladies and gentlemen, a round of applause for the often unheralded but never forgotten Dave Knopfler, John Illsley and Pick Withers. The empathy between all four musicians, in fact, is remarkable for a band so young. We've now reached the point where the superlatives should be laid on thick, in the time-honoured tradition of rock journalism. Somehow, though, it doesn't seem appropriate — though they're richly deserved — to go over the top about a band that has consciously avoided in its music all the cheap tricks and ego-tripping of rock. All I can do is recommend the discerning to ignore the fatuous advertising campaign and go directly to the heart of Dire Straits — the music. See if you can find what I have conspicuously failed to — one fault."

Dire Straits was reviewed in *Rolling Stone* in January 1979; "Dire Straits, an English quartet led by singer songwriter Mark Knopfler, plays tight, spare mixtures of rock, folk and country music with a serene spirit and witty irony. It's almost as if they were aware that their forte has nothing to do with what's currently happening in the industry, but couldn't care less. As a writer, Knopfler pens terse little narratives about the mundane problems of his brethren: women trouble, money trouble, one's-place-in-the-world trouble. He's often as clever as he is banal, so a nice line ('I need a little water of love') can be followed by a silly one ('You know it's evil when you're living alone'), or vice versa. If anything, living alone is what Dire Straits is about, and it sounds like a good life. But Knopfler isn't interested in writing songs with profound messages. In fact, the only time he tries it ('In The Gallery'), the message turns out to be a petulant attack on avant-gardism — i.e., a real yawn. No, Dire Straits get their effects by precise; well-played contrasts: the way a brisk bit of folk-rock is entitled 'Sultans Of Swing' and not only boasts an inescapable hook but also a goony, Bob Dylan-like snarl in its vocal. 'Setting Me Up' sports a standard mangled-romance theme, but the verbiage is masticated by Knopfler's growling, annoyed singing, with a giddy country-guitar solo tacked on at the end. It's a heavenly number, funny and bitter. Even when Mark Knopfler tends toward Bruce Springsteen-style street bathos in such mini-epics as 'Wild West End' and 'Lions', his band keeps everything admirably straightforward. Dire Straits is one of those quietly subversive albums whose sober lucidity reeks of rapid obscurity. It doesn't deserve such a sad fate."

Considering the point at which Dire Straits were getting started on their musical career ladder, it is perhaps surprising that they always managed to steer away from the emerging style of punk. Mark Knopfler said in 2019; "I would have been so into punk rock myself, but I was just that little bit older. I'd been playing for quite a long time, doing rockabilly, doing R&B, so I was bringing in different things. But I absolutely sympathised with punk. In terms of where it was at, where I came from. And I'd been playing in a band called the Café Racers — we were doing the same stuff, same circuit as The 101ers… I really did want to do something else. I didn't want to play Route 66, even though I was deeply in love with American music. I wanted to create a more transatlantic blues thing that was going on in my head. To sing about my own geography as much as the US'. Listening to Scottish country dance music, Celtic music and Tyneside songs, and folk as well as rock 'n' roll — it all came rushing in together. It's all tied up. For me, none of them is a foreign language."

Under the heading of "Dire Straits' Premiere Defies Disco Trend", it was considered in Tennessee paper, *The Echo* in March 1979; "It is amazing that Dire Straits' first album is selling, but sell it is — extremely well. These days, when nothing sells well unless it is pre-programmed disco with its heavy beat and simplistic melody, Dire Straits is more than a breath of fresh air. It is oxygen in a sea of methane. Dire Straits, another British group (it seems that Britain is once again the saviour in the dying art of rock music) plays dirt blues and rock in a time when rock is suffering and the blues are limited to the commercial efforts of a comedy team. On their first album, the group has cut a series of slow, lush instrumental pieces. Mark Knopfler, lead vocalist guitarist and songwriter for the band, is the brains behind the group's genius. His songs are dirty, gritty, yet highly polished, nearly perfect in execution. Knopfler's hoarse, harsh vocals play against the smooth and silky instrumentation, giving the songs an immediacy, even if the actual lyrics are only words set to the music's mood. One of the album's cuts, 'Sultans Of Swing', has become a bona fide AM hit, baffling radio execs because of its difference from the newly popular disco fad. The song, highly uncommercial, really should not sell. But this is one of those freak instances when a group is so good, so extremely better than anything else on the rock scene, that their very difference is enough to attract attention. Comparisons are hard to make with this group. When first heard, Mark Knopfler's voice is reminiscent of Bob Dylan's — the band recalls Jim Morrison and The Doors. But Dire Straits doesn't really copy any of these legendary names. Their sound is new, fresh and decidedly different from anything else being done today. The rock genre needs that boost."

"The success of Dire Straits defies the laws of musical gravity," claimed the *West Lothian Courier* in May 1979. "It proves again, that good music can prevail against the odds. The odds being behind the flash commercialism currently clogging the charts. This month sees the ten-month-old single, 'Sultans Of Swing', and the album, Dire Straits, finally reaping the rewards of airplay around the world."

It comes across that in terms of making good music, Dire Straits were in it for the long run. Mark Knopfler had told *Melody Maker* in March 1978; "We're not traditional as a band in terms of what we're producing. I don't think we're traditional in the way we think. If you write a good novel, it's considered a good novel for 1978 and the future in terms of good novels of the past."

****

Most of 1978 was taken up with extensive touring. In the early part of the year, in between a few small club gigs they toured as support to US band Talking Heads. In order to promote 'Sultans Of Swing' and their debut album, touring continued, consisting of around fifty-five performances. The tour began on 9th June 1978 at Wolverhampton's Lafayette Club and concluded on 22nd November at London's Lyceum. The whole tour covered the UK, France, Belgium, Germany and the Netherlands. The gigs outside of the UK presented Dire Straits with their largest audiences up to that point. Most of the UK venues were small halls with a maximum capacity of 1,000.

The tour saw Dire Straits perform on television programmes and overall, scale up in terms of their profile. The Knopfler brothers were clear about the kind of venues that they would prefer to play. Mark said in September 1978; "We don't want to get on the big stadia circuit. That would be as frigid as playing in an icebox. I want to play places where I've got a pretty good idea of where the back row is."

To which David added, "If you can play one big venue in a city then why not play the smaller venues and spread your appearances over several nights. We will always want to retain a warm intimate feeling so that we perform like human beings and not robots."

Combined with the rising success of 'Sultans Of Swing' and having signed a US contract with Warner Bros., by the end of 1978, Dire Straits were well known. Mark Knopfler said in May 2019; "We went out in a little minibus with Talking Heads — it was great — and got lumped in with "new wave" in the States. The Americans took to us. At first the debut album did well all over the world except the UK, because Radio One's committee had decreed that 'Sultans Of Swing' had too many words! Then it got so big in the US that they had to. I think that the head of that committee was a lady called Gladys."

The *Liverpool Echo* advocated in July 1978; "They made a huge impact on the Talking Heads tour and this album is now the icing on the cake. They are an exciting band both on stage and on vinyl and 'Sultans Of Swing' is one of the best songs to come around in ages. The other tracks all emphasise that a bright future lies ahead for Dire Straits."

Prior to touring to promote their debut album, Dire Straits had already done a number of small gigs in and around London. For some such shows, they had been the support act for not only Talking Heads but Squeeze, Climax Blues Band and Styx.

A journalist who saw a number of Dire Straits' gigs considered in *Sounds* in July 1978; "One of the most compelling of the Straits' songs is a characteristically slow, uneven hymn called 'Water Of Love', with Mark singing like Kevin Ayers over a Disraeli Gears rhythm — the chorus, slow run-downs on John's punchy bass has a catchy hook to it which raises many an eyebrow an evening. Mood is compelling, drawing you in like a whirlpool. Then there is the classic 'Sultans Of Swing', with its chunky backbeat, Clapton rendering J.J. Cale, the sort of thing you'd have been doing the Greaser dance to years ago, and yet leaving you with what Robert Christagou calls 'the jazz feeling' — a general sense of well-being rather than rock yer head off (though that didn't stop plenty of people getting into it at Middlesbrough). And the album, whilst losing the dirtiness and raunchiness of a live performance, ought to be listened to carefully — at least the oversoftness makes you concentrate on the Dylanic imagery which will explode your worldview."

Of a performance that took place at Leicester University, it was considered in the same feature; "Musical quality is the key — when you hear the Straits for the first time, or any time in fact, it takes about one song to appreciate how well they play and two or three to catch the mood. Once that happens, audience applause whistled out after every number and the hall was packed throughout. A few folks at the front were going ape shit on Mark's lead playing (he doesn't use a plectrum), others created a space for an improvised boogie to Pick Withers' immaculate drumming. The house lights were loudly booed when they interrupted the howls for a second encore. The musical appeal is really non-thematic, that is it doesn't strive to set up any confrontations but acts on instinct."

In November 1978, *Record Mirror* reviewed a performance at Sheffield University; "All credit to Dire Straits for having ignored the dictates of fashionable incompetence and brain-curdling mega-drone in favour of musical professionalism and integrity. At a time when instrumental prowess plays a subsidiary role to image and ineptitude, they have gone against the grain and established themselves as one of the year's major new acts. To be sure, Dire Straits are the only guitar band of any consequence to have emerged since the sixties. When Mark and Dave Knopfler play their instruments they strike up a dialogue both between themselves and their audience. While Blue Öyster Cult, Skynyrd and a host of others with more hardware at their disposal conduct a one-way process of stand and deliver, Dire Straits communicate and invite a more subtle response. Their guitars do not assume the role of weapons, but rather a medium through which their ideas are conveyed and statements expressed. This is particularly the case with Mark, whose lead guitar is the major part of the proceedings. He is possibly the first player since Hendrix who can make his axe speak, and indeed parts of some of the songs are reminiscent of 'Little Wing' and other tunes from the *Axis: Bold As Love* period. As with any artist of note, he realises what is left out is as important as that which is played and it is his remarkable control and delicate sense of restraint which is an essential part of his technique. The restraint evokes an atmosphere of tension which involves the listener in what is going on, inviting a kind of silent participation. Another outstanding feature of his guitar-work is his ability to play several riffs simultaneously. This produces a multi-dimensional layered effect which nevertheless remains light and spacious and without any of the claustrophobic dullness which characterises standard heavy metal routines. Such simple effectiveness appears most prominent on the newer material. 'Once Upon A Time In The West', 'Lady Writer' and 'Single-Handed Sailor' are all examples of this extraordinary effect, which relies on a combination of chord playing and finger picking. With a virtuoso like Mark at the helm, it is easy to underestimate the contribution of the other members of the band. The rhythm section of John Illsley and Pick Withers provide an excellent framework for the leads. It is the strong empathy which exists between all four musicians which enables attention to be focussed upon the guitar. Dire Straits deserved their five encores. They are heading in a very promising direction and are still likely to be going from strength to strength when ninety percent of the present fifteen-minute wonders are gone and forgotten."

In the same month, a performance was reviewed in *Sounds*; "It's obvious that I *like* Dire Straits, being ready and willing to trudge over the Pennines on a cold and blustery night to catch the first date of their tour at Bradford Students Union. In fact, unfashionable as I am, I'd class the Straits' debut album together with the Only Ones' as being the only really essential British launches of 1978. Duff production or not (I'd say not), Dire Straits have pulled off the difficult feat of ensconcing American country blues within strictly urban rock and roll and still coming up with a formula which is all their own. Intelligent, biting lyrics provide the icing on the cake, but could the same densely crafted material cut it live?"

"Funny places, Student Unions. Last gig I caught at Bradford was in the Great Hall, stiff and formal, this one's in a gigantic all-purpose chat, drink and munch mezzanine, not so much a venue as a square corridor. When the band appear on the stage in one corner the social perambulating doesn't halt, merely slows down. Not promising. They come on easy, fool around with a false start to 'Down To The Waterline' and settle down to the business of delivering the goods. I don't immediately fall about in rapture, as the Straits appear to have as much stage presence as a pint of bitter, but once acclimatised to the rather quirky sound, the set just builds and builds into momentum."

"They play virtually the whole of the album, increasing the tension so that later selections, 'In The Gallery' and 'Lions' for instance, burn with a passion which totally outstrips the recordings. But their new songs reveal an unexpected diversity. 'Once Upon A Time In The West' (riding, I suppose) is mean cowpoke stuff, guttural threats along the lines of 'Some of your mothers better lock up your daughters' punctuated with Quicksilverish guitar twanging. 'Single-Handed Sailor' includes all the appropriate nautical touches and 'They Say That He's Going Crazy' (sic) is very odd indeed, what with the drums cranked up to provide a hollow, reverberating epitaph. While on the up-tempo 'What's The Matter With You' (sic), Dire Straits — as a band, rather than just Mark Knopfler and accompaniment — begin to use dynamics much more adventurously than usual and needless to say the result rocks like a bitch. 'Sultans Of Swing', of course, is masterful Dire Straits gliding along rather than doing anything too obvious, in tune with the purist sentiments of the lyric. The bite comes in the staccato bursts Mark Knopfler slots beneath the chords. Superb. In the encore the band go one better. 'Where Do You Think You're Going?', with its abrasive, personal lyrics just builds and builds like wave motion. Having created something of a mellow cataclysm, the band disappear quietly. Dire Straits aren't much to look at, but Mark Knopfler is just about the only guitar hero I can tolerate at the moment and the others are just doing their job damn well just to keep up with him. Outside the complex the man in the hotdog van advertised 'Guaranteed, no unpleasant after effects!' I suppose he meant, only Dire ones."

It was in 1979 that that the band did their first tour of North America. They played fifty-one shows across a period of thirty-eight days. All of the tickets sold out. The success of 'Sultans Of Swing' was such that it became a strong part of their setlist.

Under the heading of "Dire Straits Are Compliment To Britain", *The Cedar Rapids Gazette* considered in February 1979; "The debut album by Dire Straits is one of the best works to come out of the British new wave scene. Carrying the group's name as its title, the record does not sound like a first attempt by a young, inexperienced band. It's a well-crafted work with a unique and distinctive sound the perfect marriage of excellent technique with authentic emotion that is neither complacent nor self-centred. Dire Straits was formed in the summer of 1977. Between then and now, the group has been racking up considerable positive reaction from both music press and the listening audience. Their material is rock and roll with an old-fashioned approach. They utilise mid-tempo arrangements with a blues and country base tailored to spotlight the guitar dexterity of frontman, Mark Knopfler. Strains of Fleetwood Mac, Eric Clapton and Bob Dylan can be heard in many of Knopfler's original tunes. Dire Straits, while equal to their new wave cronies, come off sounding like nobody else. Their music is clean with moments of flash and fire. Lyrics run the gamut from the standard love song to short stories on slices of London life. Vocals by Knopfler are strong and slightly reminiscent of Van Morrison. The diverse material on the debut Dire Straits album is hard to define. Selections included are: 'Down To The Waterline', a loping, bluesy tune; 'Water Of Love', done in the style of J.J. Cale; the angry ballad 'Six Blade Knife'; 'Wild West End', a Dylanesque piece; and 'Sultans Of Swing', a tribute to musicians not currently in vogue."

It's interesting how in the above, the journalist lumped Dire Straits in with the new wave. The band themselves and many other journalists insisted that they were not part of the new wave and just happened to be active at the same time. Still though, it's an insight into how the uniqueness of Dire Straits' music was just as fresh and as exciting as what artists more associated with new wave were doing at the time. David Knopfler told *Sounds* in July 1978; "A lot of good things came out of the new wave. But there was a lot of dishonesty about, like people hiding their age or their good academic qualifications. Your emotion has got to be true." To which the *Sounds* journalist agreed; "In contrast to many bands who opted for the easy 'we hate you' lyric and disappeared into their own pile of excrement, the present scene is down to those few who can play convincingly and keep it up, intrinsically, separate to an image."

The New York Times reported in March 1979; "'If you want to catch someone's attention,' advises a perfume commercial on television, 'whisper'. This prescription has certainly worked wonders for Dire Straits, a new English rock group whose international hit single, 'Sultans Of Swing', and first album stand out in a noisy crowd by seldom raising the volume above a murmur. Making its first local appearance Friday night at the jam-packed Bottom Line, Dire Straits proved to be one of the most distinctive and delightful bands in recent memory. The quartet's leader, Mark Knopfler, writes all the songs, gently growls the lyrics with a phrasing that resembles Bob Dylan's and plays nimble lead guitar with a light-fingered touch like no one else's. Significantly, two of his best numbers, 'Sultans Of Swing' and 'In The Gallery', sympathise with old-fashioned underdogs whose art is 'ignored by all the trendy boys.' The elegant restraint of Mr Knopfler's guitar style is not without precedents. It dimly echoes the guitar instrumentals of The Ventures, The Shadows and Jørgen Ingmann twenty years ago, and, more recently, the lazy, laconic blues of J.J. Cale. But today, Mr Knopfler's terse, tart runs and delicate shivers of vibrato are all his own. The rest of Dire Straits — which includes Mr Knopfler's younger brother on metronomic rhythm guitar — is very much subordinate, although Pick Withers is a deft drummer who jiggles the beat to disguise the uniformity of the songs' loping tempos. This, indeed, seems to be Dire Straits' only limitation: Mr Knopfler is overly fond of the same tempo, guitar filigree and even melody. But to complain about redundancy at this early stage in the band's development would be to look a gift horse in the mouth, and the freshness of Dire Straits is a gift as well as quite an accomplishment."

*8th June, 1979,
Liverpool Empire, Liverpool*

John Illsley, 8th June, 1979, Liverpool.

David Knopfler, 8th June, 1979, Liverpool.

Mark Knopfler, 8th June, 1979, Liverpool.

Pick Withers, 8th June, 1979, Liverpool.

*8th June, 1979,
Liverpool Empire, Liverpool*

*8th June, 1979,
Liverpool Empire, Liverpool*

© Alan Perry Photography

David Knopfler, 8th June, 1979, Liverpool.

John Illsley, 8th June, 1979, Liverpool.

*8th June, 1979,
Liverpool Empire, Liverpool*

© Alan Perry Photography

45

Mark Knopfler, 8th June, 1979, Liverpool.

Mark Knopfler, 8th June, 1979, Liverpool.

© Alan Perry Photography

2

Communiqué

It was after the first Dire Straits tour finished in London in November 1978 that they went straight to work on what would be their next album. The recording sessions ran from November to December of that year at Compass Point Studios in Nassau, the Bahamas. In January 1979, the album was mixed at Shoals Sound Studio in Alabama. It was produced by Jerry Wexler and Barry Beckett, both of whom were highly regarded in the field by that point in their own careers. Beckett (credited as B. Bear) also contributed keyboards to some of the nine tracks on the album.

A *Melody Maker* journalist who witnessed the Nassau recordings observed; "The mood was strained now. Mark had made several attempts to put down a lead solo on a cut called 'Lady Writer', and a slight irritation was beginning to show. Dire Straits invariably disliked doing more than four or five consecutive takes on the same song. If the pocket wasn't filled within that allotted time-span, they would drop everything, play pool and return at a later date… The prevailing spirit in Nassau was one of creative co-operation and good-natured banter. The customary demarcation lines between band and producer just didn't exist. Everyone lived together in Capricorn, a house rented from one Barbara Harkness, a millionaire patroness of the arts… Before arriving in Nassau, the band had used the Wharf Studios in Greenwich to make demos of all the material bar one song, 'Communiqué', which was written during an afternoon when engineer Jack Nuber was off sick. They recorded it the following morning… Hearing the new material (which I promised not to judge, since it hadn't been final-mixed), what struck me most forcibly about Mark's writing was its comprehensiveness. Diverse and very human emotions are given shape by an intellect which reacts to everyday events, responding to touch and visuals as well as to sound. His songs take account of atmosphere, purity of sound, sensuality, movement, change, space and tension."

Jerry Wexler brought an active interest in his role as producer. He was quoted in the same feature; "On 'Single-Handed Sailor' I can just feel myself down at the docks and hear those hawsers creaking on the swell of the tide of the Thames, and you can see maybe a green and red lantern at the end of the ship. Or the incredible picture in 'Follow Me Home' — I see cave dwellers, in the fourth century, somewhere south of Yucatan. And the music is so consonant with that."

Regarding Jerry Wexler and Barry Beckett's production, Mark Knopfler was quoted; "Everything has been done so gratefully, so professionally, there's been so much attention to detail." (Wexler had suggested that the album be titled *News* rather than *Communiqué* under the belief that the latter would perhaps sound too arty).

In terms of how he saw Dire Straits, Wexler said: "They have a southern characteristic. It's a porous, breathing track where you don't fill it all up. Making music is always a trade-off between how much you state and how much you leave to the imagination, and the answer to that is your own taste. It's impossible for me to categorise the band. There just isn't any analogue. Almost always you can put somebody into a box and say they're 'like so-and-so'. This band is not like anybody I can think of. So next step in the syllogism is don't mess with it, don't spoil it — and I don't think that would even be an option, because Mark wouldn't permit it. Mark doesn't play that kind of screaming, mindless guitar that's been so popular, which depends on just the sheer flights of the sound, but he improves melodically, which to me is the hallmark of a great musician, as opposed to just improvising within the chord structure and being harmonically oriented. He can do that and still have a familiar relationship to the song. The ghost of the song is always there. That's good improvisation in my opinion. They represent a very contemporary aspect of British society. They're young and for the most part quite well-educated people, with a very strong sense of self and where their best interests lie. There are elements of a certain consciousness, or maybe a lower-middle-class and working-class outlook with the benefit of college education, and it's very good because it's anti-establishment without a lot of blatant sloganeering. How can I put it? They respond very immediately to anything that smacks of hypocrisy or sham. There's definitely a sense of the greatest good for the greatest number. We all feel the same way, so we're not afraid to sound as if we're gushing. We really feel as if we're involved with something special. I didn't have a notion that it was going to turn out like this when we set out on this little journey."

Melody Maker's journalist who got to listen to *Communiqué* taking shape in the studio considered in his article of January 1979; "Listening to the rough mixes, every cut sounded a stone winner. It has to be said. Overall, the songs are more distinctive than on the first album and the production is streets ahead of Muff Winwood's work on the first album — which, however much the band might argue otherwise, did not do the material full justice. 'Single-Handed Sailor' evokes a crazy wind wailing round the Cutty Sark and is firm, chunky and light all at the same time. 'News' is a joyous collection of oddball phrases fronted by a beautifully picked acoustic and concluded by solitary drums, over which sneaks Mark's willowy guitar. After a loose-limbed almost-funk intro, 'Once Upon A Time In The West' settles into a loping gait with nifty lyrics. Mark decided he wanted a 'subliminal' syncopation effect on the track, so Pick and he devised a sound out of something they unearthed in the bowels of Compass Point. This 'something' resembled miniature tubular bells suspended from a piece of wood. To quieten the effect, they wrapped it up in a dirty towel. What's more, it worked. 'Portobello Belle' continues in the A-to-Z-of-London theme of the first LP's 'Wild West End', this time the spotlight falling on the celebrated open-air market. Barrow boys are a-hawking, parakeets are a-squawking while on the truck there is a wino. The central figure is Bella Donna. 'She thinks she's tough…' rings out of Mark's National guitar. Pick jokingly called 'Where Do You Think You're Going?' a 'butch song'. After an acoustic run, Mark's gruff voice spins a tale of confusion, aggression and, most of all, pain. The tempo picks up on 'Lady Writer', a compact and sinewy number that comes complete with Spanish-styled guitar break. The lady writer is on the TV, talking about the Virgin Mary. 'This is a modern beat group song,' Mark smirked. Jerry likened 'Communiqué' to Booker T And The MGs, and it includes some finely economic keyboard work from Barry. The lyrics are deliberately funny, painting a picture of someone who seems to only come alive through the memos in which he can 'say what he means'. There is a lengthy but hypnotic fade, with the rhythm and lead guitars delicately jabbing at each other. 'Angel Of Mercy' has to be the single and will probably have the new-look Rolling Stones panting a little. Its taut, exhilarating, ringing chords are matched by some splendidly tongue-in-cheek lyrics. Finally, 'Follow Me Home' slips in gently. Razor-snap percussion is met by snaking guitar and heavily anchored bassline. The primitive mood spoken of earlier emerges instantly in the words. The effect is translucent and Mark's guitar achingly understated."

The journalist surmised: "All the signs point to Dire Straits being *immensely* successful in 1979 — which means, of course, cracking America. Warners look set to pull out all the stops, for there are several reasons why the Straits must seem like a godsend to an American record company. Firstly, all the band members are personable (no office-wrecking — the gentlemanly approach makes life so much easier in the boardroom). Secondly, they're British — and Britain is still seen in America as an important talent-source. Thirdly, and most importantly, they are in the new wave without being *of* it. American record men and women hate the British new wave, mainly because they can't understand it — so imagine how those Burbank execs feel about a new British band which can be enjoyed by ears attuned to Little Feat and Ry Cooder. But their association (however tenuous) with the energy of the current British scene can only be useful. Their music appeals to such a broad cross-section of the community that Warners can dive in feet first rather than having to worry about seducing demographically-orientated programme directors of adult-orientated FM rock radio stations. It's tailor-made for freeway car radio, no less than Fleetwood Mac or Billy Joel. Just a word of warning, boys."

Stylistically, *Communiqué* continued in a similar vein to the debut album. Once again the cover art was designed by Hothouse with art directed by Alan Schmidt and the cover illustration by Geoff Halpin.

Released in June 1979 (on Vertigo internationally, Warner Bros. in the US and Mercury in Canada), *Communiqué* went to number one in New Zealand, Sweden and Germany. In the case of the latter, at the same time, the debut album was in the number three spot. *Communiqué* got to number five in the UK and to number eleven in the US. The album eventually went on to be certified gold in the US, platinum in the UK and double-platinum in France.

'Lady Writer' was released as a single. It got to number forty-five in the US and to number fifty one in the UK. *New Musical Express* reviewed it in July 1979; "So laid back we nearly damn well returned to last week's issue. Straits keep the ball dozing with 'The Sultans Of Swing — Some Further Adventures'." (Whilst no single is to everyone's taste, it is worth noting that around the time of this review, *New Musical Express* was largely championing punk and new wave bands). Besides, Mark Knopfler was quoted in *Melody Maker* in March 1978; "When people use words like laidback, it's really interesting. There's a big difference between good laidback music and music that drags after you like a giant turd. You gotta find that balance. Something may appear low-key, but it's still gotta have that tautness about it. I happen to think that craft is very important in the area of inspiration. If you're trying to inspire people, and that's the aim — to communicate — there are all sorts of qualities that are involved. The quality of craft isn't the most important quality in this band, but it is highly instrumental in producing that inspired thing, whatever it is."

Dire Straits were very self-aware in terms of acknowledging how some of the press and music-buying public weren't going to be open to some of the subtleties of their music. Regarding the wider context of how many may have engaged with music on the whole, Mark Knopfler said; "Particularly in Britain, we have a situation where most people think if a guy is playing a grand piano — short of it being Jerry Lee Lewis — it is sensitive. So that people think that Gilbert O'Sullivan, and on a more sophisticated level Elton John, are classy. And they are in a direct line from Liberace! And you can *feel* that. Elton accentuated all that in a quirky kind of way and creates something in itself out of it. But the whole thing becomes very badly bent in all sorts of ways. People are getting by with totally weak-minded rubbish and it's being lauded as highly motivated stuff. In other words, a lot of people aren't in tune. They give images of sensitivity. As a grand piano is associated with sensitivity with a capital S, so smoke bombs are associated with heavy rock. It's just the same and all that is a necessary part of the performance. The paraphernalia become very important, and I feel that's very much the case in Britain."

Since their inception in late '77, the Straits had always stood outside any of the prevailing fashions. Their reputation had grown simply out of the excellence of their music and the unassuming character of the band — the result of individual action, be it a punter hearing or seeing them for the first time or the commitment of certain people connected with the dreaded "biz". For instance, their signing to Warners in the States was effectively sparked off by the personal enthusiasm of two record company employees — Roberta Peterson in Burbank and Karen Burgh in New York. They brought the band to the attention of Wexler, the then head of A&R in Warners' East End Coast Division. The formula was repeated in a barrow-load of other countries — oddly, Britain was the slowest to catch on. Once again, individual company personnel plus local DJs had championed the first album in the face of Phonogram's hesitant official policy.

In terms of how Dire Straits compared to other acts at the time, they obviously stood at the other end of the spectrum from the massive commercial pipeline such as Kiss, or the obsessively self-centred flatulence of Styx, or even the extreme alienation tactic that was Public Image. Equally obvious is that "humanity and humility" doesn't paint a picture of deliberate self-denial or monastic self-righteousness. Their aim was enjoyment and communication on a level that combined both sensuousness and intelligence (you can dance to Dire Straits) and, consequently, they channelled everything into the music or the song at hand and abhorred the cult of the personality.

Mark Knopfler said at the time; "The real reason we're doing what we're doing is because it's real. The words that apply are love, commitment and respect. There's a lot of that on the rock scene — overcompensation for whatever's missing, which comes out as a kind of fanaticism, if you like. When you talk about that kind of fun, what you're getting is like a bicycle pump which is trying to pump up an already overinflated type. Everything's at bursting point, including the artist, and the result just isn't substantial — in almost every sense. A lot of that comes from attitude, a musician's attitude to his music."

Communiqué was reviewed in *Pop Star* in June 1979; "From the first resonant whining guitar note, you know this is the new Dire Straits album. The guitar sound is almost identical to 'Down To The Waterline', the first track of the outstanding debut album. To say they have played safe is an understatement. And although at first hearing it sounds like that's exactly what they've done, it probably isn't true — it simply comprised of another collection of Mark Knopfler songs. And great songs they are too. But it lacks the bite of their first album and their live performances. 'Once Upon A Time In The West' opens this album, with the same intro, but it doesn't roll as you'd expect, it plods. Production on this and all the other tracks is sparse, like the first album, but although it was thankful then — because it captured their live sound and the atmosphere of their music — this time, I would have liked the highly esteemed production duo, Jerry Wexler, and Barry

Beckett, to have added a bit more in the way of harmonies, and chorus, although Mr K's voice is a lot sharper on this offering."

"Leaving all those criticisms apart, a lot of this album contains fine, fine stuff. 'News', is a lovely ballad about a gambler, I believe, who makes one line in the news when he dies. And I repeat, I *think* that's what it's about. But the guitar work is gentle and sympathetic, which merely ghosts over the single drumbeat at the end — good stuff. And 'Where Do You Think You're Going?' is distinctly American, sorry, even *more* distinctly American, heavily derivative of J.J. Cale and Bob Dylan. There's sensitive ultra-light rhythm topped by distinct guitar phrasing. And the lyric, 'Where do you think you're going? I think you better go with me,' sums up a sort of lazy drifting mood, making you think of the old bronzed West Coast boy and girl."

"And finally, the title track. Again, light and funky-ish. But it slows down to ballad pace, a disappointment, as bluesy piano edges in with the melodic, rhythmic melody. So the first rocker comes on the second side with 'Lady Writer', with running guitar, some harmonies, and a bit of whoomph! Then 'Angel Of Mercy', which runs back to the blues-come-swing-come-gospel with what sounds like fifteen guitars behind one single string melody. 'Portobello Belle' and the last track, 'Follow Me Home', are predictable ballads, while 'Single-Handed Sailor' is more like you'd expect, featuring good, rolling bass and ripping guitar from Knopfler, and a bit of a progression for the band. It's a good album, but a disappointing album. If you like Dire Straits, then it's well worth having in your collection, but don't expect anything new. And get their debut LP first. For all the time and effort, I expected something better. It would be horrific if such a fine band were to rest on their laurels after such a short time."

Under the heading of "The Ordinary Alcoholic Divorcee's Band", *Sounds* reviewed *Communiqué* in June 1979; "I know you must have heard this before, but don't you think Dire Straits are aptly named? I'm not putting the emphasis on the first part of their logo, merely noting that they've titled themselves with stunning accuracy considering that their appeal lies in the fact that they invariably linger on the commercial side of despair, since *Fear Eats The Sales*, as some doomy German arsehole might have said. Rumour has it that Clive Davis, the ageing boy wonder of the American rock biz, once pronounced that Dire Straits were not suitable for the US market. We all make mistakes, and who could have blamed him for his miscalculations if they were based on a quick hearing of the band's weary, tastefully eclectic, pub 'n' grubby first album. Of course, ol' Clive hadn't reckoned on the vast market for this sort of stuff among alcoholic divorcees and "mellow" business college graduates."

"But you need to hear about the record, I nearly forgot. At the risk of being obvious, I should mention that Dire Straits have been listening to *Street-Legal* (happily, they haven't got round to *At Budokan*, yet). The rhythm section of bassist John Illsley and drummer Pick Withers have that effortless of sincere funkiness which many fools hold is only found in black chaps, and Mark Knopfler writes and plays his guitars with a subtlety that's almost boring. The other Knopfler, David, contributes adequate rhythm guitar and vocals, and the end result is like upmarket Smokie. There are no real "songs" as such, just a development of musicianship — a Mark Knopfler tune is an extension of style rather than a composition. And it works, a lot of the time. Producers Jerry Wexler and Barry Beckett keep up the Nassau sound admirably basic and cool — plush and sleepy, a complement to the cabaret jazz lead lines and the Dylanesque tales of melancholy."

"There are nine tracks, and you could have some fun with a gram of coke and a music centre tracing the echoes of Traffic, Santana and even The Doors through the maritime preoccupations of 'Single-Handed Sailor', the embarrassingly half-hearted sexiness and colloquialism of 'Portobello Belle', the final 'Follow Me Home' (a one dimensional shuffle of idyllic island passion and sundown siesta) and the title track. After two plays I started to enjoy the frigging album, so no prizes for guessing that it's going to be biggie number two here and in AOR land. I do not hate Dire Straits, in fact I admire them so much for being successful with a formula so simple that if I'm ever introduced to one of them I'll buy the pints (if they still drink them). And let's not hear any fatuous stuff about American consumers having smaller brains — if you were thirty-five and worked hard all day in Cleveland you'd bang this on and smoke some dope, wouldn't you? I mean, there's times when even I don't want to hear another loud, exciting rock 'n' roll record, but I'm not entirely sure that Dire Straits would be my choice for background moodiness. There's only one possible reason that Bob Dylan asked for two Dire Straits to play on his next album — he realises that Mark Knopfler is even more accomplished at being ordinary than he is… There are no new waves in this old ocean."

Melody Maker's review stated; "*Communiqué*, as I understand the word, issued from balance or embassy, says very little in the most elegant way possible. So elegant, so disarming in fact, that you scarcely realise that nothing has been imparted until you've read and re-read it. And this LP plays the same trick — carefully and pleasingly made, high on atmosphere but low on substance. It's a step back from the ravishing debut album, and there is, regrettably, no sign of Harry. The stories are under-developed, without the cutting imagery, it's melodically and lyrically tentative and finally, less of the same. An affecting sense of slow melancholy pervades the record — arrangements and musicianship (particularly lead guitar), are stunning throughout, but *Communiqué* is a flimsier statement, smoother and wanting in urgency and compulsion. Not so much great expectations as oblique house."

"One of the best things about Dire Straits' first album was the precise sense of place. The feel of London was often very poignant and sharp. This album, produced by Jerry Wexler and made at Muscle Shoals, is far more evocative of swamps and whisky stills. A couple of songs, about gunfighters and tired gamblers, have a cautious *Desperados* feel to them, and the token wholly London song, 'Portobello Belle', sounds like a soundtrack for a commercial about exhibiting rich Yanks to spend their summer dollars in blighty. Not that *Communiqué* isn't seductive. It's as slick as a leak from the Torrey Canyon, and in most of the songs there's a nervous feeling of being strangely menaced by menacing strangers. There is consummate rippling lead and heart-beat bass and drums, and a multi-layered intricacy that demands, and repays, attention."

"Nine songs: 'Once Upon A Time In The West' is very like 'Down To The Waterline', and the next track 'News' is similarly American in feel. 'Where Do You Think You're Going?' is beautiful — bleak, loving and grandly melodic. 'Communiqué' is a strange song of airports, rumours and flashbulbs full of blurred pictures and no comments. On the other side, 'Lady Writer' (about a recognisable erudite and pretty author) is fast and quite good enough for the earlier album. 'Single-Handed Sailor', not exactly about Francis Chichester or other round-the-world bores, is evocative of moonlit clippers and a furtively lapping Thames. It builds slowly and gets you in the end. 'Angel Of Mercy' has routine Cajun rhythms and 'Follow Me Home', with its seashore sound effects and slack drums, is moodily laid-back, but it leaves no bruises. Mark Knopfler may have received his inspiration from flicking through the *Daily Mirror*, for all these songs tell you. One set of pictures on the sleeve has the band labelled with photographers' names instead of their own. What next — the forged passports and one-way tickets to Brazil? Dire Straits, I love you, but where do you think you're going?"

In response to the this review, Dire Straits fan David Shields had his letter published in *Melody Maker* later in June 1979; "It was typical of the while cynical fickle attitude of your paper that *Communiqué* should be given a bad review. When you previewed the album a few months ago, you were full of enthusiasm for it, saying (and I quote) 'listening to the rough mixes, every cut sounded a stone winner overall, the songs here are more distinctive than on the first album.' But that of course, was before 'Sultans Of Swing', and the album, achieved the success they both so thoroughly deserved, and we all know how success corrupts and perverts — you told us. Yes, Dire Straits had now been recognised as a major new talent and you had the satisfaction of seeing your predictions all come true. But that's not where the story ends. We can't have a happy ending in *Melody Maker*. It would lose its "street credibility", or something. No, Dire Straits are now *big*, and the big boys are for bringing down. Hence Susan Hill's vague, self-contradictory and totally inconclusive review of *Communiqué*, to which her very own words could well be applied: 'Carefully and pleasingly made, high on atmosphere but low on substance' or 'full of blurred pictures but no comments.' And as for such meaningless but oh-so-clever lines as 'There's a nervous feeling of being strangely menaced by menacing strangers' — well, comment is superfluous."

"In my opinion, far too much emphasis is put on "musical progression" by the music press, until they begin to expect a band to totally change their sound overnight. *Communiqué*, to me, represents not so much a progression as a "translation" of some of the Straits' best aspects, from the raw, aggressive power of the first album to the easier, rather more relaxed mood here. Sometimes along the lines of the recent review of Ian Dury's *Do It Yourself* (a work in a less fevered dimension but still with the artist's own unique stamp) would, I feel, be a fairer comment than 'less of the same'."

"There's nothing wrong with giving an album a bad review, as long as it's done for the right reasons — i.e. it's bad. But when it just becomes a vehicle for the reviewer's apparent fondness for groaning puns ('slick as a leak from the Torrey Canyon') and when awareness of the band's success is allowed to become so prominent as to cloud her judgement, something must be wrong. And yet Susan says she loves Dire Straits. If she did, she would stick by them for richer, for poorer, for better, for worse, in sickness and in health. She loves Dire Straits *but...* Well, I love Dire Straits because they have restored my faith in good taste and justice and proved that you don't have to be Abba (or *Melody Maker*) to be successful. I'm sure that even Susan Hill (in fact, considering her love for clever wordplay, *especially* Susan Hill) will agree this has been a fair review of an unfair review of more than a fair album!"

Communiqué was also reviewed in *New Musical Express* in June 1979. For a paper that had totally got behind punk and new wave, clearly Dire Straits didn't appeal to the reviewer; "Geeing up pop paper people is a speciality of the music industry, and for at least five months — in fact since Dire Straits recorded *Communiqué* in the Bahamas — word of mouth has been that this album is 'super, magnificent, brilliant, nothing short of a classic' and so on. It's nothing of the kind. It's predictable. It's dull. It's bland. It's boring. And it's also very safe. Superficially, the formula is so similar to their excellent debut that they could arrange a substantial second mortgage on it right now — *before* it's shipping gold, as it most certainly will. It'll be a colossal smash world-wide and for the next year broadcast so incessantly that even the group will be pig-sick of hearing the bloody thing."

"And part two of a Fairy Tale Of The New Age unfolds, reading very much like the first instalment, except our heroes are much richer and more celebrated. They may even get invited to the White House and drink peasant soup. Not that I'm knocking their success — good luck to anybody who makes so much out of doing so little. And *Communiqué* is that — only three songs ('Once Upon A Time In The West', 'Where Do You Think You're Going?' and 'Portobello Belle') out of nine having any effect, and the second of those is such pure Dylan it could be hidden on *Desire* without anybody noticing."

"But it's a constricting condition of Dire Straits' appeal that you have to be fond of both Dylan and J.J. Cale, so derivative is their style. While their writer/guitarist/vocalist Mark Knopfler managed to channel these influences into a series of superb songs in

8th June, 1979,
Liverpool Empire, Liverpool

© Alan Perry Photography

the debut, here the frameworks and words show that his creative ideas are exhausted. Only 'Once Upon A Time' possesses any *real* lyrical perception — the rest is a side-stall jumble of weak and contrived metaphors, pop hooks and repetitive rhythmic chugs."

"The elder Knopfler consistently selects a series of restrained but technically superb guitar solos, spread horizontally over the lifeless backing trio, they're wasted. There's no such thing as counterpoint, interplay or *invigoration* in this operation — even the long guitar outro on the title track is bolstered by *over-dubbed handclaps!*"

"Producers Jerry Wexler and Barry Beckett must have been absolutely thrilled by the safe mundanity of it all. It's very reminiscent of the Average White Band's premature decline with *Cut The Cake*. Already Dire Straits are cosseted in an artistic vacuum, suffocated by the worst commercial aspects of their style, and Mark K has mislaid his source of inspiration. There's nothing on *Communiqué* that even *deserves* to be mentioned in the same breath of air as their debut. That's the tragedy of the new age."

"Good luck to anybody who makes so much out of doing so little," said the reviewer. Such a prophetic comment in view of what the ironic lyrics would be on Dire Straits' 1985 hit, 'Money For Nothing'.

The *Daily Mirror* said of the album; "Dire Straits are still a relatively new group but on this, only their second album, their classy music makes them immediately identifiable. One of the albums of the year."

****

Communiqué would prove to be the last Dire Straits album to feature David Knopfler. He left the band in August 1980 during the recording of their third album. After the recording sessions for *Communiqué* had been completed, Dire Straits went on tour for pretty much the rest of 1979. They started in Rotterdam in February (so four months prior to the album's release) and did a total of one hundred and sixteen shows across Europe and North America until their final concert in London on 21st December.

With several people making references to Bob Dylan as an influence, it was perhaps no surprise that the man himself checked the band out at their last performance at the Roxy in Los Angeles on 29th March. Dylan had already heard 'Sultans Of Swing' and was so impressed that he asked Mark Knopfler and Pick Withers to play on his next album, *Slow Train Coming*.

With the US leg of the tour concluded in early April, Knopfler and Withers went to Muscle Shoals at the end of the month to record the Dylan album. It is unlikely to be a coincidence that Dylan had brought in Wexler and Beckett to produce it. Neither of them, nor the Straits' guys were initially aware that Dylan was to make a lyrically religious album.

Knopfler voiced his concerns to his manager, Ed Bicknell, remarking that "all these songs are about God," but he was also impressed with Dylan's professionalism. "Bob and I ran down a lot of those songs beforehand," he recalled. "And they might be in a very different form when he's just hitting the piano, and maybe I'd make suggestions about the tempo or whatever. Or I'd say, 'What about a twelve-string?'"

****

It was advocated in *Gibsons Coast News* in May 1979; "We should all be familiar with Dire Straits by now. Their first album has been out for more than six months and it nearly went unnoticed until someone actually listened to it and decided to take a chance and play it on the radio. Now it is firmly rooted in the top of the album charts and the radio playlists as well. The success of Dire Straits shows that people want to hear something other than the soft disco pap that is currently strangling the radio frequencies across North America and the radio programmers are starting to respond. Their songs are longer than those of most new bands but the energy is there in abundance as well as a bit of punkish venom. Their second album *Communiqué* is to be released in May and the band could be in the unique position of having two albums in the top ten at the same time; I would like to see their royalty cheques if that happens."

Despite Dire Straits' success, they were still very private and reluctant to talk about themselves. It was even harder for the press to persuade them to interpret their own music. Personal biographies only stood in the way of appreciating the music, they argued, while one of the most vital aspects of their approach was to keep a song open-ended, with a life of its own, as independent of its creators as possible.

Mark Knopfler said at the time; "I feel more of a detachment now from "me" in a song, which doesn't *detract* from the song. It's just a rock song. I don't feel that I should have to answer for it — I'm not trying to negate my own responsibility for them completely, but there's a whole load of natural good licks that take on a life of their own, in terms of their cohesiveness, yet still leave all kinds of open ends for chance or whatever might crop up. I think that applies to a lot of people who write and play. There's a sense in which songs are like other people. You can't own them, or say that *this* is what was intended, because you'd be a liar. It's contradictory, I know, because the whole thing is coming from you anyway."

"But when somebody does a portrait, for instance, I'd be very surprised if the level at which it comes out resembled what they photographically intended, if you like. It's a nice discovery to make, actually. I don't know if you've ever found that a thing that might begin to take shape of its own accord, either by the dictates or the formulae that you've decided to use or just through the sheer multiplicity of the content, or I don't know what. What I'm saying is that you've never got anything mapped out completely. Given that, I think what you do need is a feeling of format, but what I really want to avoid is all the personal attention on Mark the bloke, who is *just* a bloke. I really don't want any of that shit."

"Sometimes when I listen to these songs, I think 'That's got nothing to do with me as a bloke.' For instance, 'Follow Me Home' — a new song — is important in a lot of ways. Yes, I was on an island, and yes, there was a girl — but it's not very different from any other tourist sleeping on a beach, going up to a ruin, looking out over the sea, eating meat and drinking wine. But the idea goes beyond that, leading to a song which doesn't actually belong to the bloke. I like to be divorced, in that sense, from the song."

Back on the road and in June 1979, *Pop Star* reviewed the Glasgow Apollo show; "Everything about their live act is so casually precise. They wander onstage as though they'd taken a wrong turning coming back from the loo, and without so much as a 'hey, there's a lot of people out there looking at us', they're into 'Down To The Waterline'. Not as immediate as the album version, and any early sparkle not easily apparent. They find their groove though with 'Six Blade Knife', Mark Knopfler's piercing lead guitar stabbing through the solid backing, and on to the first new song of the night 'Once Upon A Time In The West' — a song in the Dire Straits mould, the only real description I can offer."

"Okay, so Dire Straits have stamped their trademark on the rock scene with a unique guitar sound and a would-be sophistication, but Knopfler's lead vocals are on occasion too perilously close to Dylan's for comfort, and the same basic guitar sound becomes very, very wearing after three or four numbers. A rough comparison could be, don't laugh, someone like Smokie. They hit the charts originally with a ditty sung by a vocalist who sounded as if his larynx had been manicured by iron filings. A winning formula they soon realised, and God knows how many hits later he's still singing in the same fashion to a variation of their original melody. By their fourth or fifth number they'd did everything they were gonna do. Mark Knopfler had squeezed the sharpest note from his guitar, sang his gutsiest vocal, and the band had blended their best harmonies."

"Indeed, onstage they rely entirely on their musical output because their stagecraft amounts to zero, and the other three band members do little except fill in the basics in their respective departments — especially drummer Pick Withers. They closed with an inferior 'Sultans Of Swing', the vocal falling far short of the recorded version although a superb piece of lead guitar saved face, and 'Wild West End', as low key a climax as you're ever likely to stumble across."

The interesting thing about this review is that on the surface, it appears to be what most would consider a bad one. However, delve a little deeper and the reviewer has actually complained about things that, to many, are good points about Dire Straits, their music and their stagecraft; none of it was trying to be gimmicky or in-yer-face. It was straight-up good music and really, perhaps that is something that made the band stand out so much compared to some of the other high-profile acts who were popular at the time (especially in terms of punk and new wave).

A performance that took place in Liverpool was reviewed in *North Wales Weekly News* in June 1979; "Isn't it funny how something you expect to be so good often turns out to be a big disappointment. I got that feeling watching Dire Straits at Liverpool Empire on Friday. The phenomenal success of their first LP in America — it's the biggest-selling debut album ever from a British band, including The Beatles — seemed to point the way to something special. So did all the coverage they have received in the music press. But alas, Dire Straits seem to have fallen victim to their own rocket rise. Their set was more like a club act than a band headlining a tour of major theatres. The main fault wasn't so much the material, but the unbalanced order in which the songs were performed. Consequently, there were periods of their performance which I found dull."

"Don't get me wrong, I think that the Straits are excellent musicians, with two good albums in the debut LP and *Communiqué* — but there was just something extra missing. Mark Knopfler gave an excellent Eric Clapton/Lou Reed/Bob Dylan style performance vocally, but he didn't have the stage presence of any of these artists. Pick Withers, who has risen from playing drums on Welsh language records only a few years ago, gave an excellent steady performance. From time to time he got so carried away that he fell off his drum rostrum. The band excelled on numbers like the funky 'In The Gallery' and the slower 'Once Upon A Time' and their performance accelerated as soon as they began to play their hit single 'Sultans Of Swing', which got an ecstatic response from the crowd. After this their performance was spotless. Some interesting lighting and good public address system helped them win the crowd over. At the end of the day that nagging doubt about the band remained. But who knows, in a couple of years they might just find the missing key."

It comes across that the reviewer was expecting something more theatrical but really, was that kind of thing within the Dire Straits remit in 1979? It seems that they were more about the music in and of itself and whilst that plausibly garnered a few less-than-elated reviews, it certainly got through to the fans who embraced and welcomed the band for what it was.

In the same month, *Sounds* reported on a performance that took place in Birmingham; "It's no casual whim that Dire Straits' promotional badge and logo is simply a Fender Strat with the band's name scripted over it. For a Fender is substantially what this band are all about, the Fender that rests in the nimble and inventive hands of lead guitarist Mark Knopfler."

"Now that's not meant to decry the vitally important contribution made by the rest of the band, who represent the perfect foil to Mark's crystal clear virtuosity, but without his unique finger-picking style I'm sure the Straits would never have scaled the dizzy heights at which they currently stand. He is certainly a long way from the stereotyped axeman of either old or new, with not a plectrum in sight and his fingers twanging out the notes almost flamenco style (a technique I've seen only Roy Buchanan successfully employ before) and giving his solos both an irresistible attack and an intriguing texture. He nurses and caresses his guitar, then cajoles and strangles it while it bucks and weaves in his grasp as if alive."

"An overly fanciful description? Well perhaps, but I defy anyone who is lucky enough to be toting a ticket to this sold out homeland lap of honour by the Straits not to be impressed by Mark Knopfler's almost casual captivity of the stage. Support band Metro had been specially chosen for this tour — not, as sometimes happens, because they would offer no threat to the headliners, but because the Straits genuinely liked them, and I can see why. They bridged the difficult gap between today's popular ice-cool chic and the more straightforward ramablam of conventional rock 'n' roll (largely due to the contrasting roles played by the frigid featured vocalist Peter Goodwin and the titanic thunderings of drummer John LaForge)…"

"Mark Knopfler was an object lesson in how to dominate a stage without resorting to over-the-top flamboyancy, never failing to give his solos gusto as well as guile and finally leaving the arena after no fewer than three encores bathed in both glory and sweat. Okay, so his vocals were often garbled and unintelligible, but that is as much a part of the overall Straits sound as John Illsley's unflappable bass lines, Pick Withers' inventively underpinning drumming and David Knopfler's all-important rhythm accompaniment. The set itself was perhaps a predictable mixture of the phenomenally mammoth debut album and its already equally successful follow-up, with the likes of 'In The Gallery', 'Wild West End' and (of course) 'Sultans Of Swing' rubbing shoulders with 'Once Upon A Time In The West', 'Single-Handed Sailor' and 'News'."

"But what else can you expect/want? I know what so many people say about the Straits — they're so laid-back they're virtually horizontal — and I agree their albums may not exactly be tailor-made for setting your stereo alight. But live, that's very well a different matter. Onstage, they are quite simply a rock 'n' roll band of towering proportions (both visually and aurally). And isn't that what it's all about?"

Dire Straits had become one of those rock myths that some of the music press didn't quite trust — from Clapham to platinum in less than a year, the pub rockers who conquered the world. Their Hammersmith Odeon gigs were probably the most eagerly awaited shows of the year. Their tour was sold as a triumphal homecoming — the crowds gathered to greet these local lads who'd stunned the States. But for some this myth fudged the issue. Accidents don't happen, and what's interesting about the Dire Straits story isn't in the success but its surprise. In retrospect, there's nothing odd about Dire Straits' American sales at all. Their music is so obviously American that the post-*Communiqué* critical consensus fingered Dire Straits as hip easy-listening already. The band apparently become bland even quicker than they became big. Such sour grapes don't solve the problem either.

What is interesting is not why Dire Straits made it, but why they didn't. People trot out the 'Sultans Of Swing' story too glibly: 'Sultans' became an American hit, therefore it became a British hit too. A misleading "therefore". Everyone loved 'Sultans Of Swing' the first time they heard it. What the Straits' US success changed was not the fans' minds but those of the marketing men. Dire Straits suddenly had credibility. The British sales push began, belatedly, in earnest.

The question is why the Straits weren't credible from the start. Why had their subsequent sales been acclaimed as "incredible"? And this isn't a musical matter at all. The Straits' problem was image — they didn't come across the way potential superstars, from Thin Lizzy to The Clash, are *supposed* to come across. The British music biz is obsessed with style and label, and Dire Straits slipped through it like pick-pockets through a fancy dress parade.

Dire Straits' Hammersmith show that year was remarkably slick and remarkably plain. The group did everything a class group does. They had an elaborate lighting pattern into which everything was made to measure. They played two fake encores. They featured a guitar hero and an adventurous drummer (plus drum solo). Mark Knopfler ended each song with the rock star's practiced leap — hit the stage and the music stops. His inter-number patter was studiedly inarticulate. This was a very professional show. But also a disarming one. Fans arrived cold and left warm. Dire Straits, for all their lighting crew's hard work, still didn't come across as stars — they could, still, have been playing the local. Dire Straits' stage was clean — no banks of technology, no crouching acolytes.

In a review of the Hammersmith show, a *Melody Maker* journalist said, "I arrived after the show had begun, and the band were already boxed in by their lights. It was as if we were peeping into a rock fantasy — push the button and the group begin to play, push the button and the crowd begins to clap. This was a very *decent* gig, the way things were, once upon a time, supposed to be."

Dire Straits' success was not unprecedented. Ace's 'How Long' sold the same mood, the Average White Band made a similar (if slower) move from London clubs to American masses, and the previous year's US summer hit was 'Baker Street', Gerry Rafferty's trustful account of London loneliness. What these artists had in common was a post-adolescent rock commitment.

On their debut album, Dire Straits made, very effectively, music for London's flatland — melancholic, curious, observant. The interesting contrast is with Steve Gibbons' *Down In The Bunker*, an album with similar references and concerns (and an album that was panned in Britain, praised in the USA). His music was cruder than Knopfler's, but more obvious in its realism, with posed toughness — it rocked more than it swings. But Gibbons, like Knopfler, celebrates the ordinary.

At the time of Dire Straits' ascendancy there were still hundreds of sixties musicians left — weaned on The Shadows, blooded on the Stones, matured on Dylan. By the mid seventies these people had become teachers, social workers or under-employed graduates. But they still dreamt of the days when they had dreams.

As *Melody Maker* put it at the time: "It's a fleeting dream, and Dire Straits' may be a fleeting success. *Communiqué* sounds as good as *Dire Straits* but it has much less to say, and it's unclear yet whether Dire Straits will get marooned in American business music. The Dylan connection doesn't fill my heart with joy, but it does make the story complete — Dylan is, after all, *the* fantasy friend of a whole generation of rock fans. I hope it isn't the end though, just as I hope Dire Straits won't be confined to the rags-to-riches myth. I mean, that was the *easy* bit."

The continuing references and association with Dylan appeared in the press again, after the European tour concluded in early July. Dylan's *Slow Train Coming* was given a bad review in *Record Mirror* in August 1979, largely due to the lyrical content following Dylan's self-declaration as a born-again Christian, which saw comments like, "every track herein spouts fourth holier than thou pomposity and has the overall effect of turning one away from Bob Dylan."

But the contribution from the Dire Straits' guys was given praise: "Every track here preaches and fights the good fight and, although the Dires and Co. play remarkably like Dire Straits, the overall work is completely unlistenable as a complete entity."

In the same month, *Sounds* put similar emphasis on their review of *Slow Train Coming*: "'I Believe In You' is a simple, relatively unadorned hymn of faith. If you're feeling very cynical you'll call it a slushy travesty of 'She Belongs To Me' but for all its nicely rounded corners and fluid clean solo from Mark Knopfler to settle you still further back into the cushions, you still have to contend with Dylan's rough-edged warblings that give it a sense of conviction."

That said though, *Sounds* were more positive about the album overall, finishing their review with "After just a few plays, every track except the last has registered positively for me. And I can't say that for more than half a dozen albums this year."

✲✲✲✲

In November 1979, *Rocksound* reported on a gig that took place at Chicago's Uptown Theatre on 7th October where Dire Straits were on the bill with Ian Gomm: "As impressive as Gomm was, the real revelation of the evening came with Dire Straits. The band apparently has set out to become more animated and forceful onstage and, happily, has hit its target. The danger with this sort of self-conscious shift is the tendency towards forced emotions — which is what singer/guitarist Mark Knopfler succumbed to early on as he grimaced for all he was worth, staggered about the stage and choked the hell out of his guitar — but the heat the group finally generated left the posturing in the dust. Delivered at a slightly faster speed than usual, with Pick Withers' syncopated drumming playing of Knopfler's fluidly convulsive leads to maximum effect, 'Sultans Of Swing' positively took off. The set's other bit of magic was provided by 'In The Gallery', which was given a hard, rapt treatment that made the recorded version sound tame by comparison. Only 'Twisting By The Pool', a playful new rave-up, failed to satisfy, it found the group somewhat out of its element. Knopfler's Dylanesque vocals are wonderfully effective in the context of Dire Straits' gritty street songs, but he is not particularly strong on flat-out rockers, a failing that surfaced again at show's end. Indeed, the man who should have been singing 'Nadine' and 'Gloria' with Ian Gomm, who instead remained in the background, half-heartedly strumming his guitar and looking rather uncomfortable. Too bad: as a result of Knopfler's spotlight-hogging, a superb concert ended not with a shout but with a sigh."

In December 1979, as a sign of the band's increasing popularity *Melody Maker* reported on a performance that took place at Gothenburg's Scandinavium; "The Straits, with the experience of loud-mouthed, rowdy, exhibitionist, media-pumped American audiences behind them, are used to something more than the glacial frenzy of the Swedes, but sitting behind the mixing desk it was difficult to decide where the freeze set in — with the band or the audience. The Straits played long — twenty-one songs — and certainly loud enough for the carpeted ice stadium, but their over-familiarity with much of their material and the lack of breadth and contrast in the set left the evening like a limp tightrope — high at each end, but sagging ominously in the middle. Two new songs were immediately worthy of attention — 'Solid Rock', which sounds like the Stones caught in mid-funk, and 'Twisting By The Pool', a worthy rock 'n' roller that owes its final appeal to Pick Withers' Sandy Nelson drums and Mark Knopfler's jiving guitar — but neither could be seen to twitch a Swedish toe, and the superior studio demo tape of 'Solid Rock' that was played to the emptying hall halted none of the hurrying fans. The set now reeks of routine and the performance is a solid, competent compromise between the touring need of another day, another show, and the musicians' need to hold back some protection against the wearing limits of rock life. The set slowly regained tension, especially when the kicking rhythms (they need many more) of 'Solid Rock' fed into 'Where Do You Think You're Going?' when Mark played beautifully full-veined guitar. While British fans will be anxious to see the Straits in the next few weeks, the band desperately needs time to rest, to write, to find out exactly where they're headed. At the moment, they're circling elegantly in a vacuum."

Mark relaxing pre-gig at the Stadthalle, Freiberg, West Germany, 2nd June 1979

With the dawn of a new decade on the horizon, Mark Knopfler told *Melody Maker* in November 1979; "The eighties will be a bit of a lucky dip. People will realise even more the limitations of labels — they'll realise that they are their "own" wave. And a lot more people who were around, out of the limelight but oiling the machinery, are going to come to the surface. I think that's going to be particularly true on the radio, people who were denied airplay in the sixties and seventies will start to get it. I think there'll be more regional stars. The influence of European musicians will be felt more on a world basis, but it's still remarkable that a band like us can work all over the world and sell records all over the world. If you're willing to work at it, you can make a lot of impact all over the place."

Mark, 11th June, 1979, Birmingham

© Alan Perry Photography

11th June, 1979,
Birmingham

© Alan Perry Photography

Mark Knopfler, 11th June, 1979, Birmingham

© Alan Perry Photography

David Knopfler, 11th June, 1979, Birmingham

*Pick Withers,
11th June, 1979,
Birmingham*

© Alan Perry Photography

11th June, 1979, Birmingham

© Alan Perry Photography

Mark Knopfler, 11th June, 1979, Birmingham

John Illsley, 11th June, 1979, Birmingham

David Knopfler, 11th June, 1979, Birmingham

© Alan Perry Photography

Mark Knopfler, 11th June, 1979, Birmingham

John Illsley, 11th June, 1979, Birmingham

Mark Knopfler, 11th June, 1979, Birmingham

© Alan Perry Photography

83

Mark Knopfler, 11th June, 1979, Birmingham

David Knopfler, 11th June, 1979, Birmingham

Lewisham Odeon, December 1979

Dire Straits as part of an all-star line-up, alongside Eric Clapton and members of Thin Lizzy, Led Zeppelin, Bad Company and Supertramp at the launch of the The Summit compilation album. The artists donated tracks and the royalties to help raise money for sick and handicapped children.

Making Movies

As soon as the *Communiqué* tour finished, Mark Knopfler set to work writing songs for the next album. It would see him working on that stage for the first half of 1980. Having heard Jimmy Iovine's production on Patti Smith's song, 'Because The Night' — a song co-written between Smith and Bruce Springsteen — Knopfler was keen to work with Iovine. Iovine had already worked on Springsteen's *Born To Run* and *Darkness On The Edge Of Town* albums, and as part of this, he would be instrumental in recruiting E Street Band keyboardist Roy Bittan for Dire Straits' *Making Movies* recording sessions. Mark co-produced *Making Movies* with Iovine at the Power Station in New York between June and August 1980.

There were four songs from the sessions that were not released on the album: 'Making Movies', 'Suicide Towers', 'Twisting By The Pool' and 'Sucker For Punishment'. In January 1983, 'Twisting By The Pool' was released on the *ExtendedancEPlay* EP, which hit the UK top twenty.

During the recording sessions for *Making Movies*, Mark and David Knopfler had several heated arguments. When tensions between them came to a head, it saw David leave the band over creative differences to embrace a solo career. Illsley was quoted in *Rolling Stone* in November 1985; "David was under a lot of strain. Mark felt very responsible for David and didn't quite know what to do. But once *Making Movies* was out and David had left, it seemed to lift a tremendous strain. Mark felt very freed."

Regarding his brother, Mark Knopfler said in *Rolling Stone* in January 1983; "One of the problems was having this huge, great spectre of a big brother writing tunes and telling everybody what to do with them. It's probably much better that I should leave him to grow up in his own way. I certainly wouldn't want to tell him how to do that."

Two years later Mark expanded on what led to David leaving the band; "I think the main thing is that I'm naturally cut out to do what I'm doing. And I'm not sure whether Dave is… I mean, Dave was never into guitar as much as I was. Dave plays only keyboards now… It's cool. I don't see much of him, really, just because we're in different countries… We've always been able to speak to each other. I played on his first solo record. I was concerned with going on. I knew what I wanted to do. The other guys could come or not."

Perhaps the way in which things scaled up so rapidly for Dire Straits was something of a surreal experience for David. During the period of working on *Communiqué*, he had said, "This is my first real rock 'n' roll band, apart from the odd weekend here and a couple of days there when I was much younger. Here I am, less than a year after signing a deal, sitting in Nassau talking to you — ginger ale, fag, half a million albums under my belt, second album being produced by two of the best producers going… I just get excited about how well things are going. There's always plenty of good news to counterbalance anything that might be a bit difficult. It's like a big balloon that keeps on floating up."

David Knopfler wasn't credited on *Making Movies*. It was reported in *Circus* in January 1981 that whatever guitar work he had contributed to the album had been erased prior to it being mixed and mastered. With David out of the band, the recording sessions continued with Sid McGinnis on rhythm guitar and keyboardist Roy Bittan (a classically trained musician, and already well-known for his work with Bruce Springsteen).

Notably though, David appears on video playing 'Solid Rock' and 'Les Boys' live in concert. Those performances preceded the *Making Movies* recording though. Sid McGinnis was also uncredited on *Making Movies*. Overall, the line-up changes in Dire Straits saw them expand into a quintet when keyboardist Alan Clark and guitarist Hal Lindes were recruited as permanent members.

Having undertaken some training and exams in classical piano playing, and having played in Geordie with Brian Johnson (who became AC/DC's frontman), Alan Clark had been recommended to Mark Knopfler's management by the manager of Gallagher and Lyle, for whom he had played for on tour and a yet-to-be-released album.

Clark told the *Newcastle Journal* in December 1980; "I joined just after they (Dire Straits) came back from the States where they recorded the latest album. It was rather rushed because we only had two and a half weeks of rehearsal before the tour started… It was easy because they're all great guys. Socially everyone gets on very well. It was a lot easier than I thought it would be actually, because when I got the phone call and Dire Straits was mentioned, I couldn't imagine them with keyboards. But then I heard the album and basically half of it was written on keyboards really because Mark is starting to play piano."

Alan Clark had spent two years planning and preparing for his first solo album when he received the offer that would mean putting it all on ice. Even though all that work was just starting to come to fruition, the freelance musician had no hesitation in opting to shelve the project. The reason? Mark Knopfler had invited him to join the multimillion selling band, stepping into the shoes of Bruce Springsteen's keyboards man Roy Bittan, who had provided the keyboard work on *Making Movies*.

Reflecting on events decades later, Alan Clark said to *Ultimate Classic Rock* in May 2014; "A friend of mine was a big Dire Straits fan, so I'd heard quite a lot of their music. Obviously, I'd heard 'Sultans Of Swing' on the radio and stuff like that. He used to play the albums every time that I was around his house. I was working with a variety of different people. I was working with a duo called Splinter who were signed to George Harrison's label. One of the other people I was working with was Gallagher and Lyle — they had a series of big hits in England and possibly in the States. So I was working with them (also) just before joining Dire Straits. Dire Straits had cut the *Making Movies* album and Mark was adding keyboards — he had Roy Bittan from the E Street Band play some keyboards on the record. Mark was very interested in bringing in a keyboard player, so they asked around and one of the people who was asked was Gallagher and Lyle's manager, who recommended me. So in a way, I was kind of headhunted. I went along and played at the rehearsal and never came back (to Gallagher and Lyle), basically."

Mark Knopfler told *Circus* in January 1981; "I didn't have to do that much more work for this album even with Dave gone. I always did play a lot of guitar. It's just a matter of playing the songs over again — on lots of songs you do that. On the Bob Dylan record (*Slow Train Coming*), I might have done two rhythm guitars before I even started to put on lead guitar. The real reason *Making Movies* took six weeks to make instead of three is that Shelly (Yakus) was so meticulous in getting Pick's drum sound right."

Only in the previous two years had Mark Knopfler been in a position to call the shots in a major band. Working with a technician of Iovine's calibre would have seemed a remote possibility in the Hope And Anchor pub days. Mark had just left a fulltime teaching stint and was new to fulltime rock. While a sensitivity to language still informed Mark's songwriting, he claimed that rock, not teaching English, suited him best.

Three of the seven songs from *Making Movies* — 'Romeo And Juliet', 'Tunnel Of Love', and 'Solid Rock' — would go on to make a significant contribution to the setlist for later Dire Straits tours (*Love Over Gold*, *Brothers In Arms* and *On Every Street*). Also from *Making Movies*, 'Expresso Love' was included in the setlist of all Dire Straits' tours up until 1986.

Making Movies signified the point at which Dire Straits moved towards making longer songs of greater complexity in terms of arrangements. In an interview for the *Aberdeen Evening Express* in November 1980, Hal Lindes said; "I must admit I was very surprised when I first heard the new album. I thought there had been quite a development in the sound. My personal opinion was that here we had a sort of matured Dire Straits."

In view of how *Communiqué* had been mostly written off by many as just more of the same after Dire Straits' first album, *Making Movies*, was quite crucial to their continued success and their credibility as a creative force in contemporary music.

The San Francisco Examiner said in November 1980; "Knopfler's most familiar piece of reportage is still 'Sultans Of Swing', the song about a provincial jazz band that made Dire Straits' first album a best-seller. The British band's second LP, *Communiqué*, was criticised for sounding a great deal like the first album, which it did, but its sales around the world were still impressive. *Making Movies*, the group's recently released third album, is something of a departure. On the first two records, Knopfler's conversational singing and reliance on basic guitar-band instrumentation were reminiscent of some of Bob Dylan's early rock and roll recordings, a comparison that was further underscored by Knopfler's occasional use of Dylanesque vocal inflections. The new album sounds more like Bruce Springsteen. Jimmy Iovine, who produced *Making Movies* with Knopfler, and the engineer, Shelly Yakus, have both worked with Springsteen. The album features the keyboards of Roy Bittan from Springsteen's E Street Band. But the sound of the record, which is richer and has more punch than previous Dire Straits albums, isn't the only point of comparison. Several of Knopfler's new songs 'Tunnel Of Love', with its carnival imagery, and the urban street scenes of 'Romeo And Juliet' skirt close to Springsteen's territory, and the theme of lost love and lost innocence that threads through the album is one of Springsteen's main preoccupations."

"But perhaps one shouldn't make too much of this comparison. Knopfler is one of the most distinctive rock guitarists in recent years, and while his vocals are looser and more varied here than on the band's earlier recordings, they're still highly personal. And Springsteen would never have taken a line from an Elmore James blues as the starting point for a new song, as Knopfler does on the new album with 'Hand In Hand'."

To which Knopfler was quoted, "I like to start from a point like that and bring it up to now, but often you do things when you're writing and you really don't know why. There's a lot on this record like that. Towards the end of 'Hand In Hand' there's a guitar figure that sounds like the song '24 Hours From Tulsa'. I didn't realise that until after we'd recorded it. Sometimes I write something without precisely knowing the meaning; in a situation like that, the writing is more instinctive."

Making Movies was released in October 1980 on LP and cassette. It was first released on CD in 1984. The album stayed in the UK charts for five years where it peaked at number four. It got to number nineteen in the US and to number one in Italy and Norway. The album was later certified platinum in the US and double-platinum in the UK.

Released as a single, 'Romeo And Juliet' got to number eight in the UK. 'Tunnel Of Love' was featured in the 1982 Richard Gere film, *An Officer And A Gentleman*. Although the song only got to number fifty-four in the UK when released as a single in 1981, it is one of Dire Straits' most well-known songs. Its introduction features 'The Carousel Waltz' by Richard Rodgers and Oscar Hammerstein II.

Compared to some of the other Dire Straits' songs, 'Tunnel Of Love' is more complex in terms of its length and overall arrangement. Knopfler said in *Rolling Stone* in November 1985; "It's in different sections, but there's a kind of logic to it. It seemed like it needed that breakdown section in the middle with the drums, trying to convey the big swinging movement, the screaming and the noise. It all stems from extending an idea. You can use circus music as a device to put you there, where there's a smell and a feel, a geography where people can have their own little stories, be in their own little movie."

Making Movies was reviewed in *Record Mirror* in October 1980; "More scintillating than *Star Wars*! More action than *Apocalypse Now*! part three of Deptford Against The World — staring Mark Knopfler and his trusty sidekicks Big John and Pick. Special guest appearance by Roy Bittan. John Wayne would have loved Dire Straits. Keen as an arrow, they made it on their own terms. Knocked down by the press who feted them and then kicked them in the teeth, they shrugged their shoulders but never buried their heads. Yes, it was easy to sling mud as they churned out yet another version of 'Sultans Of Swing'."

"I hated the second album recorded in the sleepiness of Nassau. At that time Straits seemed to be trading on their past success. But let the lights go up and the trumpets blast. This is the big one. The title is very apt as Straits' songs have always sounded like film scripts — the bloke off his motorbike or the band struggling to make headway. Deptford's answer to Springsteen have also enlisted the man's keyboard player and went off with a book full of ideas. Preceded by a grainy old movie theme, we're at least led to the stuttering backbeat of the first song 'Tunnel Of Love'. At first glance it's pretty standard Straits, until Bittan is let off the leash for the first time, nudging into the song with a mini-instrumental that stands out on its own. 'Romeo And Juliet' echoes like a busker down in the tube tunnel. A bleak track that disappears quickly in a mass of semi distorted guitar."

"'Skateaway' is presumably the tale of a girls fantasy while skittering around on roller skates and plugged in to the headphones. It seems to be the track that Knopfler enjoys the most, swinging in at six o'clock with your senses firmly in his sights. Bittan again sweetens the honky tonk of 'Expresso' while Knopfler plays more vocal games appearing least when expected. 'Hand In Hand' and 'Solid Rock' wallow a little, but 'Solid Rock' whiplashes back — initially sounding more Stones than the Stones before heaped guitar breaks kicking and biting. I saw Straits debut the final track 'Les Boys' at the Rainbow last year. It was a theatrical piece and a mighty piss take, that has lost nothing in the recording studio."

New Zealand's *Rip It Up* review in December 1980 said; "Jeez, talk about snatched from the jaws of defeat! Another album like *Communiqué*, and Mark Knopfler may have had to drag out the typewriter and start working for a newspaper again. Knopfler, producer Jerry Wexler and the boys in the band had got so *tasteful* with the songs on *Communiqué* the album had the sting of an Andy Williams' greatest hits collection. *Making*

Movies brings in a new producer, Jimmy Iovine, who was on the panel for Tom Petty's *Damn The Torpedoes*, and Roy Bittan, Bruce Springsteen's piano player. Both make life-saving contributions. Iovine provides a rough, interesting mix, which washes away the instrumental predictability that had become so boring. Bittan's beautiful rock and roll keyboards virtually become the lead instrument, giving Knopfler the freedom, which he seizes, to get away from all those recycled J.J. Cale licks. To top it all, Knopfler has got some bite into his singing, and written songs that avoid cleverness in favour of plain feelings. The tired edge of disgust he brings to Juliet's quote in 'Romeo And Juliet' — 'Aww, Romeo, yeah, I used to have a scene with him' — packs more emotional punch than all the songs on the first two albums. Listen to any track on *Making Movies* and prepare to be startled and delighted."

Circus advocated in January 1981; "The record's content balances Knopfler's fluent, intricate guitar playing with his tautly-written evocations of impassioned experiences. Each song benefits from alternately kicky and subdued Iovine/Knopfler production, as well as a new-found flair for composition on Mark's part. The nocturnal settings of many of the lyrics, along with Knopfler's breathy singing, impart a sensuousness to *Making Movies* that the first two albums barely began to explore. The sensuality is a strong ingredient in the formula that makes Dire Straits so potently intriguing, especially for America. 'If they hadn't worked so hard on this record,' says a high-placed industry observer, 'the physicality of John, Pick and Mark might still be eluding American rock fans. The kids here only think of the pretty boys of rock because that image is what's being marketed. American kids respond best to what Mark calls 'pretty strangers' in his song ('Romeo And Juliet'). Look, the difference between a cuddly pop star and Mark Knopfler is like the difference between Cheryl Ladd and Anna Karina. One is playing a role with a toothpaste smile, the other has real warmth and presence, and has been popular in Europe for some time. Now Mark and the boys are really spelling their presence out — like in 'Tunnel Of Love' — so nobody can miss the message, and it looks like the audience is buying it.' Worldwide acceptance of the new material such as 'Skateaway' and 'Solid Rock' supports the impresario's claim. A few artists, including Graham Parker and Bruce Springsteen, have proven that they don't have to be pretty and plastic to make saleable rock and roll. Add Dire Straits to the list."

The album was even reviewed in *Harrow Midweek* in October 1980; "On their first album, Dire Straits sang lovingly of the seedy, romantic side of London. International success saw the group, and frontman Mark Knopfler in particular, take a broader, less Londonised view of life on their second album, *Communiqué*. *Making Movies* has the group firmly settled in America — an America reminiscent of Bruce Springsteen street life and love songs which tear at the emotions like a knife. It's a beautiful album with some spine-tingling imagery and at times some very hard-rocking music. But Dire Straits were once hailed as an English band, singing English songs — will they ever take a walk in the Wild West End again?"

And in the *Liverpool Echo*; "'The sound is overall grittier than ever before' says the press handout. And there you have it. A grittier Dire Straits reworking their way through something old and something new with people like Springsteen's keyboard player Roy Bittan giving them more depth and scope on tracks like 'Skateaway' and 'Romeo And Juliet' which are likely to become the best known tracks from an album that shows they can still have some claim to be the Sultans of Swing."

The *Newcastle Journal* said; "By far the best and most varied of their three albums. Opens with rocking reflections of Whitley Bay 'Tunnel Of Love', cools down for 'Romeo And Juliet', builds and subsides on 'Skateaway', 'Expresso Love' harks back to 'Sultans Of Swing'. 'Hand In Hand' is emotional, 'Solid Rock' packs clout."

And in the *Reading Evening Post*; "Dire Straits' first album was the right one at the right time — the band's melodic rock approach was welcomed when everything else seemed avant garde. The second effort was a mite disappointing. Now we have the third — *Making Movies*. In terms of musicianship it's marvellous, of course, but I have doubts about its style. The producer and keyboards player have both worked with Springsteen and the influence is obvious. Personally, I think The Boss does it best and the plagiarism route is a cul-de-sac."

In the same month, the *Belfast Telegraph* reviewed the album; "As there are only a dwindling number of shopping days left before Christmas, many people will no doubt be looking around for suitable presents for those near and dear to them. They might even be considering buying an LP. They might consider, for instance, buying *Making Movies* by Dire Straits, who are a very popular band and will be here in January. This LP is not for your head-down mindless boogie persons. No, this is one for your discerning rock fan. Dire Straits are the good old Sultans of Swing themselves and their latest offering reveals them at their best — just taking it easy and getting it right. The musicianship on *Making Movies* is excellent and the lyricism way, way above the average. Coarse people will describe this as boring and old hat, but they would be wrong. This LP has charm as well as passion. It reveals a band who are concerned with and believing in rock music as an art form. They have provided a lyric sheet again with their LP and it helps you appreciate the powerful imagery of this band's songs. The opening track — 'Tunnel Of Love' — is of fairground romance — love on the dodgems as it were, and includes some brilliant lines."

Rolling Stone reviewed *Making Movies* in February 1981; "Singer, songwriter and ace guitarist Mark Knopfler is the impressive sum of several very appealing parts. His voice is a smoky mixture of Bob Dylan's acidic whine, Tom Waits' tubercular snore and J.J. Cale's breathy, marbles-in-the-mouth whisper. He writes such songs as 'Sultans Of Swing' and 'Once Upon A Time In The West' with the cinematic flair of Bruce Springsteen, the hall-of-mirrors imagery of classic Dylan and the slashing thrusts of Neil Young's bayonet-like realism. Finally, Knopfler's guitar style is a shotgun wedding of jazzy chording and harmonic tangents descended from Django Reinhardt and Wes Montgomery, the no-nonsense electric blues of B.B. King, Jimi Hendrix' string-bending sensuality and James Burton's country-pop sheen."

"On Dire Straits' first two albums, Knopfler wore his influences proudly on his sleeve. But when he pinned them on the band, they stood out like scarlet letters. *Dire Straits* and *Communiqué* were like roll calls of the star's patron saints, yet all too often Knopfler's hero worship overshadowed both the richly romantic tapestries of his tunes and the tasty team playing of bassist John Illsley, drummer Pick Withers and now-departed rhythm guitarist David Knopfler."

"On *Making Movies*, Mark Knopfler pushes back those influences, rolls up his sleeves and knuckles down to the business of cutting a Dire Straits disc that's far greater than the sum of its parts. 'A house of cards…' he admits in 'Solid Rock', the snarling, guitar-driven number that best describes what the new record is all about. Indeed, compared to his crystalline elegance and fragile introspection on the first two LPs, the creator of *Making Movies* now seems as bold, confident and determined to take chances in life, love and rock and roll as the brassy rollerball queen he watches with such fascination in 'Skateaway'. On this album, Knopfler is making "movies" — i.e., songs, some of which remind us of films: *Carousel, Romeo And Juliet, West Side Story, Cabaret*, et al. — not just acting them out."

"And what a difference the right producer makes! On 1978's *Dire Straits*, Muff Winwood simply succumbed to the bleached-out tonalities suggested by the cold, misty blues of 'Down To The Waterline' and the lurid yet limpid pink-neon afterglow of 'Wild West End.' (On the import LP *The Honky Tonk Demos*, Dire Straits' own scrappy 1977 eight-track demo of 'Sultans Of Swing' conjured up the composition's carnival atmosphere better than their Winwood-produced hit single did)."

The review continued, "For *Communiqué*, Jerry Wexler and Barry Beckett merely enriched the R&B textures in the group's sultry sound, marching Knopfler's instrumental chops into the breach at the expense of his material and the sorely underrated rhythmic tension between Illsley and Withers. Jimmy Iovine, who co-produced *Making Movies* with Mark Knopfler, succeeds where the others failed: he builds the album from the songs up. True, the addition of E Street Band pianist Roy Bittan brings out colours that were only implied in David Knopfler's workmanlike strumming on *Dire Straits* and *Communiqué*. But it's Iovine who puts all the pieces together here: gritty guitar runs, muscular drumming and bass playing, sympathetic keyboards, sensitive and assertive singing."

"Then, after the groundwork has been laid and the shots set up, Mark Knopfler steps forward to star in and direct each highly emotional but never cheaply melodramatic scene. Knopfler fires most of his big guns on side one, which begins with a riveting, eight-minute romance called 'Tunnel Of Love'. Bittan's opening quotation from Rodgers and Hammerstein's 'Carousel Waltz' quickly metamorphoses into a brief, cascading piano figure that carries us straight into the boardwalk world of middle-period Bruce Springsteen. There, amid the deafening roar of roller coasters, cars and people who are frantically racing toward nowhere, a young man and woman find safety and solace for a few precious hours."

"But where Springsteen would probably have turned their love into a grandstand play, Knopfler simply takes what he can get and lets it go ('I could have caught up with her…'). Throughout 'Tunnel Of Love', Mark Knopfler dramatises this close encounter by using his guitar as a Greek chorus. The singer practically spits out the early verses while dodging his own instrumental licks as they ricochet against Illsley and Withers' solid wall of sound. Later, as Knopfler walks alone through the 'carousel and the carnival arcades,' waiting for another night and another girl, he wraps his voice like a ratty old raincoat around Bittan's gently tinkling piano and the long guitar solo that ends the track. Somehow, the evocative moan of the artist's guitar suggests a truth much deeper than the carnival-as-life metaphor has revealed."

Still from the same review: "As fine as 'Tunnel Of Love' is, *Making Movies*' masterpiece is its second song, 'Romeo And Juliet'. For once, Knopfler's words coalesce into something more than a mood, a clever skit ('Les Boys') or a neat vignette ('Skateaway'). Lyrically, he breaks through and makes us care, even cry, for the street kid who's lost his girl because her dream of success came true and his didn't (though they shared the same dream). Now she doesn't need her lover anymore, and when he comes around, she crushes him with her casual 'hey it's Romeo… what you gonna do about it?' All he can do is realise that she's suddenly in another league, that she thinks of him (if at all) as little more than a comic figure from her past. In the choruses, Mark Knopfler reaches peaks of passion he's never before attained… But, of course, such pleading is useless — tragic, devastating, even funny, yet ultimately useless."

"We're moved, but the subject of the song certainly isn't. Musically, Knopfler cradles 'Romeo And Juliet' with a tender melodic reprise from Bruce Springsteen's 'Jungleland', which he plays beautifully on a National guitar, giving the tune the timeless feeling of, say, Rod Stewart's 'Mandolin Wind'. There are no hot lead-guitar breaks here. Roy Bittan's piano keeps to the shadows while the rhythm section maintains a soft shuffle, jacking it up for the potent choruses."

"The combination of Jimmy Iovine's understated production, Mark Knopfler's incredibly powerful singing and the strength of the story itself make 'Romeo And Juliet' the greatest victory on a record not lacking in triumphs. Two of *Making Movies*' other compositions are also boy-meets-girl numbers. 'Hand In Hand' explores ground similar

David Knopfler quit during the recording of Making Movies to focus on a solo career.

Hal Lindes, Mark Knopfler, Pick Withers and John Illsley in discussion at Phonogram Records, London.

Step forward Hal Lindes. His debut tour in 1980.

102

to 'Romeo And Juliet' but can't begin to match the latter's force."

"In the randy and exhilarating 'Expresso Love', however, Knopfler is so knocked out by the intensity of his relationship with his girlfriend (expressed in a cup-of-coffee metaphor!) that he can't wait to gulp her down again. 'I don't want no sugar in it,' he shouts. 'Thank you very much.' 'Solid Rock' finds the singer in an affirmative, philosophical mood, ready to straighten out both his life and his music with a healthy dose of "solid rock". 'Skateaway', a marvellous miniature, could serve as an anthem to roller skaters everywhere, while 'Les Boys' — a strange and surprising anticlimax on an album this good — trots out cabaret, apparently just for the hell of it."

"Guitar freaks who genuflected over every riff on *Dire Straits* and *Communiqué* may be disappointed at what seems like a shortage of rave-up Knopfler solos on *Making Movies*. There are a few (in 'Tunnel Of Love' and 'Solid Rock'), but the beauty of the artist's current playing is that each note and phrase is woven into the fabric of the tales he tells. Unlike the other LPs, this one boasts songs, not solos. More important, *Making Movies* is the record on which Mark Knopfler comes out from behind his influences and Dire Straits come out from behind Mark Knopfler. The combination of the star's lyrical script, his intense vocal performances and the band's cutting-edge rock and roll soundtrack is breathtaking — everything the first two albums should have been but weren't. If *Making Movies* really were a film, it might win a flock of Academy Awards."

In 1981, a short film (also called *Making Movies*) was released on VHS and Betamax, as well as screened in some theatrical venues. It consists of music videos for 'Romeo And Juliet', 'Tunnel Of Love' and 'Skateaway'. They were directed by Lester Bookbinder.

1980 saw Dire Straits nominated for two Grammy Awards; one for Best New Artist and one for Best Rock Vocal Performance by a Duo or Group for 'Sultans Of Swing'. Mark Knopfler was also praised for his performance on Phil Lynott's *Solo In Solo* album. *Record Mirror* advocated in April 1980; "Dire Straits' guitarist Mark Knopfler has stamped his distinctive mark on 'King's Call' and although you could say the result sounds more Straits than Philip, I think you'd be missing the point. It's a superb song and could be another contender for a single."

****

With *Making Movies* complete, now as a quintet, Dire Straits embarked on a tour of Europe, North America and Australia. It was referred to as the On Location Tour. The tour concluded in Luxemburg on 6th July 1981. Under the heading of "Keyboard Player Adds Dimension", it was reported in the *Newcastle Journal* in December 1980; "The addition of a keyboards player has certainly given hitmakers Dire Straits added depth and width in their stage act. This fact was not lost on last night's packed Newcastle City Hall audience who showed full — and richly deserved — appreciation to a performance which even surpassed last year's fine effort. Geordie Mark Knopfler is still kingpin in the band — writing all the material, playing lead guitar and taking lead vocals — but Alan Clark's work on electric piano and synthesisers fills out the sound on an excellent team effort. This was especially noticeable on their massive hit 'Sultans Of Swing', which sparkled with an extra vibrancy — the nostalgic looks at childhood trips to Whitley Bay's Spanish City on 'Tunnel Of Love' and the latest single, 'Romeo And Juliet'. The enthusiastic fans were treated to the range of tracks from the new album *Making Movies*, their third and finest to date — 'Expresso Love', 'Skataway' and 'Solid Rock' all evoking warm applause. Mark proved himself a witty raconteur when relating how a hungry trip to a Munich penthouse disco, where the cabaret act was truly dire though hardworking, inspired 'Les Boys' for the LP. In fact, the interlude served to underline the only fault with their stage presentations — lack of chat. However, it did not really matter when they dished up such early delicacies as 'News', which Mark dedicated to the late John Lennon. 'In The Gallery', 'Once Upon A Time In The West', the reminiscing 'Down To The Waterline' and the requested encore, 'Wild West End'."

The success of the performance overshadowed earlier concerns over ticket sales. It had been reported in the *Newcastle Evening Chronicle* in November 1980 that "Two of the North East's biggest superstars return to Newcastle City Hall in the next few days — but both must be a little disappointed at the response. Ticket sales for both Yes and Dire Straits have been surprisingly low" but that Dire Straits "seem to be unfairly suffering at the hands of some critics these days after reaching huge heights of popularity around the world eighteen months ago. It's a case of the music press delighting in building bands up to a peak then knocking them down. But, to my mind, the new album, *Making Movies*, is a stronger all-round than either the great debut LP or the disappointing follow-up, *Communiqué*. In particular, the marvellous opening track, 'Tunnel Of Love', is a nostalgic look at childhood haunts such as the Spanish City, Whitley Bay, and Cullercoats, is the nearest Mark has got to the exhilarating heights of his all-time rock classic, 'Sultans Of Swing'. 'Skateaway' is another fine track and the guitarwork throughout is as superb as ever."

It was reported in the *Belfast Telegraph* in November 1980: "Dire Straits are one of Anne Nightingale's guests on *The Old Grey Whistle Test*. The band has achieved considerable success since its early days when it was quite literally in such dire straits that the members decided to use it as their name. The success of singles like 'Sultans Of Swing' and albums like *Communiqué* have changed all that and the band is now a sell-out wherever it goes."

And in the *Aberdeen Evening Express* in the same month; "Dire Straits, the millionaire band with a destitutes name are to turn the clocks back three years to the days when they were scraping for a living in the small clubs around Britain. Although they have received sixteen platinum discs and twenty-one gold for their first two LPs, they plan to hit the club circuit on the American leg of their world tour. Their customised coach will flash past the big stadiums that have been the standard venues for big name bands from Britain and take them around the streets and corners to the smaller clubs."

To which Hal Lindes was quoted; "We are keeping it down to club gigs. Personally I am knocked out doing these places. It will feel like starting all over again. It will not only get us closer to the audience but will bring the band together. When you are playing that type of gig you have to know exactly what each band member is going to do next."

It was a prospect that would have horrified the band in November 1977. When the hard economic facts of life had led them to choose their name, Dire Straits was the reality!

The Birmingham Odeon gig was reviewed in *Record Mirror* in December 1980 (note that the comments in brackets hereafter are from the reviewer!); "This is the first tour by the Straits since the lesser known Knopfler brother, Dave, left earlier this year, to be replaced by Hal Lindes on rhythm, the new five-man combo completed by Alan Clark on keyboards. So what of the new Dire Straits? If you like the old Dire Straits, you'll like the new 1980 version as well because it's still Mark Knopfler and friends. He's probably the best guitarist in the world for all I know but surely that doesn't give him the right to dominate every single song (I use the term loosely). In 'Romeo And Juliet', a modern (sic) love song, he uses a pinpoint beam reflecting off his axe to dazzle and blind everyone (does the light really shine out of his guitarse?). It's a nice effect but only the occasional burst from Clark's keyboards arouses any interest by now. There's a song for John Lennon, 'News', then of course 'Sultans Of Swing', which is dragged out and on and on to be followed by 'Skateaway', 'Tunnel Of Love' and 'Angel Of Mercy' which all have an uncanny resemblance to 'Sultans Of Swing'. In fact, I'm sorry to say it, but in two hours only one song stood out as being different. 'Les Boys', a clever musical cameo based on a gay cabaret act in Germany with a Dietrich intro and strong melody content. It's comparable to 'Une Nuit A Paris' by the old 10cc and is just as accurate, precise, clever and, well, different! Dire Straits are strictly a rock band, none of this pop nonsense for them. They are a proud anachronism, stubbornly travelling in a different time warp, carrying thousands along with them. The crowd like it (I think), no one danced in the aisles, there was no mass adulation. Everyone remained dutifully seated throughout and applauded in all the right places. It was strictly circa 1970 all over again and who am I to say that is a bad thing? However, they must eventually move on and if 'Les Boys' is the direction they're heading then maybe there's hope, if not, Dire Straits could well become a predicament as well as a name."

In December 1980, it was reported in the *Aberdeen Evening Express* that "Dire Straits played an excellent set at the Capitol on Sunday with a bunch of old favourites as well as material from their new album *Making Movies*. No matter how laid back they may sound on record, in live performance they pull out all the stops. Mark Knopfler was on top form."

The European tour would have been followed by a trip to Japan, but this was cancelled because drummer Pick Withers' wife was expecting a baby. Then it was off to Australia and points east, touring until the end of July, upon which they were due to start work on the next album. Mark had already started composing for it.

Alan Clark said; "I've already heard one track called 'Telegraph Road', which he has played at soundchecks. It sounds really good. It's about this road which goes on, absolutely straight for about fifty miles, which we drove along into Detroit while we were touring the States. I think it could make a single."

Regarding Mark Knopfler's writing of 'Telegraph Road', Clark was quoted in *Ultimate Classic Rock* in May 2014; "'Telegraph Road', he actually wrote it bit-by-bit when we were on the road. At every soundcheck for every gig afterwards, he and I would get together and we'd sort of formulate the next bit of the song. He'd written where we'd gotten up to, and we would then start making it work between us with the piano part and his part and that's how the song was built up. I was actually present when he started writing it, which was sitting in the front of a tour bus during the *Making Movies* tour when we were heading to Detroit because the Telegraph Road is actually a road that runs into Detroit. We were driving up that road and it's a big, long, straight road and I recall it had one slight kink in it, but other than that it was perfectly straight and it went on for miles and miles and miles into the city of Detroit. The whole song was based around that journey and how somebody else might be making that journey in the early days when the road wasn't there and how the road came about. So it just fired Mark's imagination, sitting in the front of the tour bus."

Mark Knopfler told *Melody Maker* in October 1982; "The song is just a combination of circumstances. We were actually on the Telegraph Road in Detroit, on the bus, and I was sitting there, and this road seemed to be going on forever — the motor industry was really run down then. I was reading this *Growth Of The Soil* book, and the song is a combination of the book and the place I was at. It's a bit movie-esque, for want of a better word — there are longshots and we'd talk about the middle instrumental section as the movie section, because you'd feel that the camera would pull away and you would get a view of things as they were and as they are now. It's like a film with its own people and little trains and trucks, a lake and fields and buildings. I'm not massively fond of it, but there it is. It just got done."

Performing at the Teatro Ariston, Sanremo as part of the Sanremo Music Festival in February 1981

Love Over Gold

With touring complete and with 'Telegraph Road' already composed, Mark Knopfler set to work writing the songs for Dire Straits' next album. It would be the last to feature Pick Withers (Withers would later be replaced by Terry Williams. Williams had been in Rockpile as well as several other Welsh bands, including Man).

It was between March and June 1982 that Dire Straits recorded *Love Over Gold*. Mark Knopfler produced the album and Neil Dorfsman engineered. It marked the beginning of what would be a long line of collaboration between them.

Love Over Gold was largely characterised by jazz-rock fusion, but it also included orchestral arrangements that helped to make it unique. Neil Dorfsman — who also engineered on Knopfler's 1983 *Local Hero* soundtrack — was quoted in *Sound On Sound* in May 2006; "I think Mark was at a stage in his career where he was looking to do something other than straightforward rock music. He was always interested in doing a lot of different things. I remember him studying jazz and really woodshedding a lot on his guitar at home, and it knocked me out how adventurous he was, trying to expand his horizons. He just loved jazz and that whole New York scene."

Knopfler told *Melody Maker* in October 1982; "The boring bit — as a musician, I don't know whether I get any better as a writer at all. For instance, if you learn a new chord one morning out of a book, then as a writer I would straightaway start to use it. I just take advantage of that extra knowledge and put it to work. I don't actually have a hunger for musical training — I can't read music or anything — but everything I learn I use. So it comes out in songs like 'Love Over Gold'. It means that you can advance. I'm really looking forward to the next few years. I keep falling in love with music all the time."

For the *Love Over Gold* recording sessions, Knopfler used a range of guitars; four Schecter Stratocasters — one blue, one sunburst and two red — a black Schecter Telecaster and Ovation twelve and six-string acoustic guitars. He used an Ovation classical guitar on 'Private Investigations' and 'Love Over Gold'. On 'Industrial Disease' he used a custom Erlewine Automatic. On 'Telegraph Road' he used his 1937 National steel guitar.

A number of songs that were written and recorded during the making of *Love Over Gold* didn't make the final cut. 'Private Dancer' is one such example. Once all of the vocal tracks had been put down, Knopfler considered that a female voice would be better suited to the song. He gave it to Tina Turner for her comeback album which was consequently called, *Private Dancer.*

John Illsley was quoted in *Musician* in September 1985; "We were going to put 'Private Dancer' on *Love Over Gold*, but in the end I don't think Mark really wanted to sing it; it's really a woman's song. Tina heard a very rough tape and loved it so much she asked if the band could play on it. It was tremendous fun. Tina came in and recorded it live in the studio with the band. She gave it three hundred percent energy. You'd think she was in front of 20,000 people rather than four guys. We were putting down the tracks."

Mark Knopfler didn't play on the track, he had other commitments and so Jeff Beck came in to play the guitar solo, but the other Straits agreed to record with Tina Turner.

In response to being asked what the differences were between Dire Straits' and Tina Turner's version of 'Private Dancer', Alan Clark was quoted in *Ultimate Classic Rock* in May 2014; "The arrangement was different. That's essentially the major difference. I think Tina might have done it slightly faster. But I played on Tina's record, so I sort of brought the keyboard parts and in fact, John played on it — and I think it was pretty much the Dire Straits band without Mark that played on it from what I recall. So we pretty much brought it over. But the producer, whose name was John Carter, had basically revamped the arrangement to make it a bit more of a single, I guess. But other than that, it was pretty close to the Dire Straits way, because we had recorded it with Dire Straits. Obviously, it sounds a bit strange with Mark singing it, which is why it never got any further. But other than that, it was kind of very similar, really."

Knopfler used 'The Way It Always Starts' on his soundtrack for the film, *Local Hero.* Gerry Rafferty did the vocals for the song. It was considered in *Rolling Stone* in November 1985; "Knopfler's 1983 soundtrack for the Bill Forsyth film *Local Hero* conjures up vivid images of the Scottish Highlands with its pensive melodies and the solitary sigh of his guitar."

Love Over Gold is abundant in long songs containing lengthy passages, many of which strongly showcase Alan Clark on piano and keyboard. Regarding the album, Clark said in 2014; "It was great because Mark sort of gave me carte blanche, really. He was very interested in writing and incorporating keyboards into the band, obviously. So I just jumped on the piano and started doing my shit, so to speak… We spent a fair bit of time rehearsing and constructing the arrangements of the songs. Dire Straits have always been meticulous about rehearsing. Mark and I both agree that the rehearsing is the most enjoyable time of the whole process, because it's totally creative and it's like anything goes. You get such a buzz from creation that it was a joy to rehearse, whether it was rehearsing to make a record or rehearsing for a tour or even rehearsing midway through a tour."

It was reported in *Rolling Stone* in January 1983; "While it has traditionally been the mission of most British bands to set their sails full-tilt toward the US in search of a big score, Knopfler does not see himself as a world-beater. In fact, *Love Over Gold*, whose lead cut runs nearly fifteen minutes long, is an album that seems designed to torment quick-fix American radio programmers. And when Warner Bros. Records asked him to edit the endless cut — a dramatic survey of the socioeconomic landscape called 'Telegraph Road' — into a five-minute single, Knopfler declined."

To which the guitarist was quoted; "I don't think something like that is worth an answer, do you? The only thing you can do is be a nice English chap and say no thank you."

'Sultans Of Swing' had come out in the States when disco held such sway that Warner Bros. — Dire Straits' US label — had devoted a whole floor to it. And consisting of five tracks spread over forty minutes, *Love Over Gold* was released at a time when three to five minutes was the standard in terms of song length.

Appealing to the US was perhaps not a primary goal at the time. Manager Ed Bicknell told *Rolling Stone* in January 1983; "Dire Straits is a gold act in the US. To become a platinum act, we'd have to spend all our time plunking around there. These are guys in their early thirties; they're starting to settle down, get married. If we play Greece or Portugal, we're an event. If we play Boise, Idaho, we're probably the tenth band through there that month."

Speaking to *Melody Maker* in October 1982, Knopfler said; "As far as pop or the radio goes, none of my friends listen to the radio and I don't. New York doesn't even have a jazz station anymore — can you believe that? I think it went country, which means that it went pop because country music stations don't play country, they play Eddie Rabbitt, who's a pop singer really. That's okay by me. As far as I'm concerned I'm happy that people wanna dance and sing. I just carry on and do the best I can... Record companies are the last people to pressure us, partly because we're so successful and we're paying their wages to a certain extent and subsidising a lot of their other acts. I think in America though, the attitude of the record companies is silly. In Los Angeles, they have the idea that if a record doesn't sound like the Doobie Brothers... That cliquey A&R/producers set-up is labouring under the illusion that they have got a finger on the tap of what pop should be like. And in fact it's nothing like that. They just turn out this boring Christopher Cross thing. The last thing they asked me to do was edit 'Telegraph Road' down to five minutes. That's where they're at. That shows their understanding. Fortunately, we're in a position to tell them what to do. We've let them bring out 'Industrial Disease' so they can get it played on the radio. They stand up and claim that they're giving people what they want but of course everything comes down to some kind of denominator. They talk about whether you will test well or not. So your hand may be pumped one day by some arsehole who says 'You're testing very well, you might be interested to know'."

Indeed, opting to play it safe for commercial appeal didn't seem to be the be-all-and-end-all either. In January 1983, a journalist writing for *Rolling Stone* advocated of Knopfler: "A superb guitarist in a traditional style and a songwriter whose tunes take little account of passing trends."

Love Over Gold was the first Dire Straits album to be produced solely by Mark Knopfler. The title of the album was inspired by a piece of graffiti that he had seen in London out of the window of his old council flat.

In Europe, 'Private Investigations' was released as the album's lead single. The single got to number two in the UK, their first top five hit single there. A noteworthy success considering that the song comes in at just under seven minutes long. Atmospheric and full of character, it went on to become one of the band's most popular songs live and went on to be played as part of the *Brothers In Arms* and *On Every Street* tours.

Knopfler said of the song in 1982; "I think that 'Private Investigations' is partly about writing songs. It was sparked off by something that I'd read about Philip Marlowe. Basically he's on the side of right but generally speaking up against it and trying to do something positive in an extremely bitter environment. Chandler's world was LA, which was always kind of bleak. Still is. A strange place, an unnatural place. The song is a little bit tongue-in-cheek. It's amusing. You hear different interpretations of it, but to me it's deliberately a movie. A little soundtrack really. I don't think it's any big deal — it's just what was there. It's not intended to mystify people. I had this Italian-style movie tune. I was playing acoustic guitars because I wasn't working with the band at the time. And I had a movie

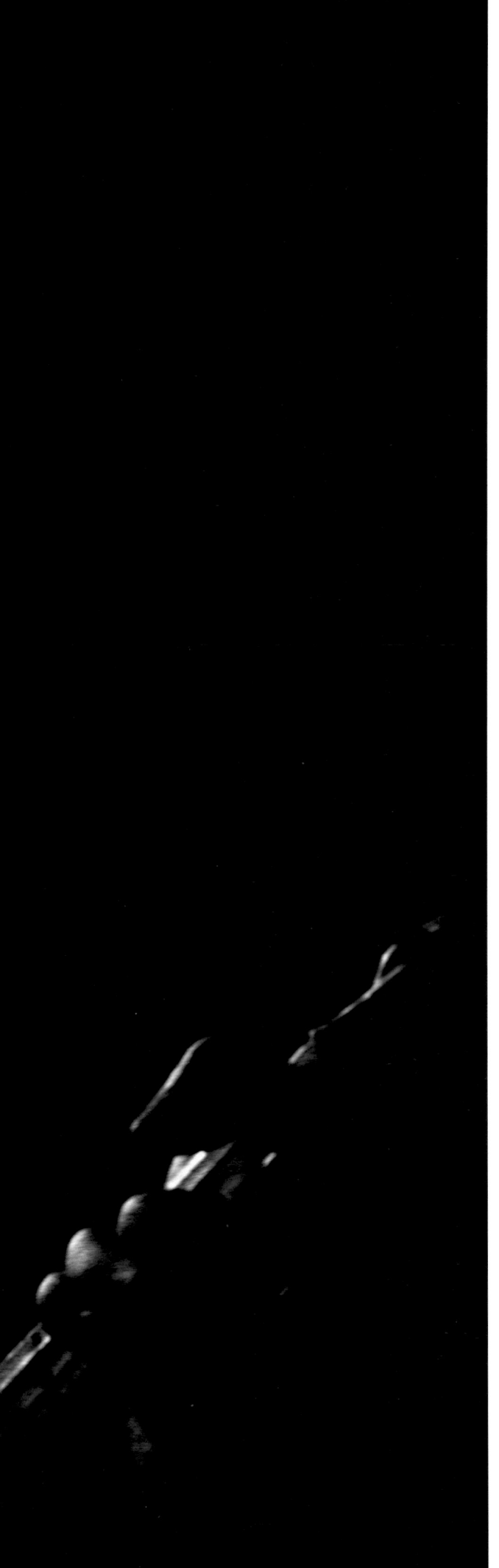

*Mark Knopfler in full flow at the
Ijsselhal, Zwolle, Netherlands,
12th June 1983*

score coming up so I was doing that kind of thing anyway. I had this other instrumental piece and they were both in the same key. They just went together so well. One of the things about being a writer is that you just use things. The random nature of the universe is connected to the random nature of songwriting. There doesn't seem to be much of a formula to me. Every song has a life of its own. I mean, sometimes you put something in because it rhymes. People would like to think that it is much more profound than that but that's not the case, because basically you might have gone to a rhyming dictionary."

Following the opening track of 'Telegraph Road', 'Private Investigations' was an unusual offering from Dire Straits compared to their other songs up to that point. Knopfler was quoted in *Record Collector* in May 2019; "It was peculiar, yes. The record game wanted another single, so I thought: what's the least likely on the whole thing? That was just sheer obduracy from me. The next thing I knew, DJs were playing it and the very fact that it was so different had got everybody talking about it. I was experimenting in the studio. Using footsteps, breaking glass on the floor, just — using sound. Parts of that are just me heavy-breathing! So it was basic psycho-acoustics. Stuff I probably wouldn't bother with now, but was good fun at the time."

The B-side of 'Private Investigations', 'Badges, Posters, Stickers And T-Shirts', is an equally unusual offering. Quirky. A track that wasn't included on *Love Over Gold* but certainly worth its due all the same. In the US, 'Badges, Posters, Stickers And T-Shirts' featured as the second track on the *ExtendedancEPlay* EP.

It was reviewed in *Melody Maker* in October 1982; "Dire Straits are swinging now. They're bopping. My God, they're even twisting! They've just spent three days in the studio recording a three-track EP as unlike anything on *Love Over Gold* as, well, the first album is from the fourth. Back to the roots, if you like, back to the good ol' rock 'n' roll of 'Eastbound Train', back far beyond the mega productions of *Love Over Gold* to the good-time music that was sweated out five years ago on the tiny stages of the Hope And Anchor and the Rock Garden, when the encore was a frantic version of Chuck Berry's 'Nadine'. Quite a change of style."

Knopfler said; "I just love the old EPs. Maybe the album was a bit heavy duty, a little bit intense. People talk about epics and masterpieces and it all makes me feel a bit urgh. I don't really like epics myself. Those tracks are like horrible monsters. With the EP, I think it's kind of nice to have songs that are warm and maybe have happy endings. My favourite kind of records are like Sam Cooke's 'Having A Party'. I was really inspired by Chuck Berry's 'You Never Can Tell'. You get the impression that a lot of people are anxious, they're insecure, they're depressed about the state of things, and it's kinda nice that you can hold up the idea of two young people meeting, and you've gotta keep on wishing people the best, hope that they'll have a family and be happy. It just kept bugging me and bugging me and all of a sudden I woke up and it burst and I said 'Right, we've got to go into the studio and do this'."

In February 1983 Fordham University's *Observer* asserted: "Dire Straits, which recently released their fourth album, *Love Over Gold*, have come up with a fun little EP that is the first recording with the group's new line-up. Backing Knopfler is ex-Rockpile drummer Terry Williams on drums, American Hal Lindes on guitars, Alan Clark on piano and John Illsley (the only original member left, besides Knopfler) on bass. The first cut, 'Twisting By The Pool', is a party rocker if ever there was one — a far cry from some of the stylistic, brooding material on *Love Over Gold* — and bristles with energy. Williams shows off his straight-ahead percussion kick with a short, thundering solo. On the second side, Mel Collins joins in on saxophone for the equally up-tempo 'Two Young Lovers' (another great dance song) that is right in the Rockpile, Nick Lowe school of pub rock. It's the kind of song in which a corny lyric such as Knopfler's 'It was the last day of summer…' seems perfect for the music. The EP closes with the pretty, mid-tempo 'If I

Had You', featuring a sixties type groove and those 'Sultans Of Swing' guitar flourishes that are Dire Straits' trademark. This EP points to what the band has been calling a Dire Straits rebirth. Everything is lively and inspired and doesn't sound too much like earlier albums. If you can find the record, at low EP prices, it's a good buy."

Back to the album, as the shortest track on *Love Over Gold*, 'Industrial Disease' references a number of concepts that were relevant to the manufacturing industry at the time regarding strikes, depression and an overall lack of cohesiveness. It was the main single from *Love Over Gold* in Canada where it was a top ten hit. The single got to number nine in the US on Billboard's Hot Mainstream Rock Tracks chart. It got to number seventy-five on the Billboard Hot 100 in 1983.

Of the final track on *Love Over Gold*, Knopfler explained; "'It Never Rains' — that doesn't really have anything to do with anything, it's just kind of a grotesque. I remember starting it almost as a doodle just because 'seven deadly sins' rhymed with 'terrible twins'. It just sort of got bigger and bigger and bigger. It just grew into this dream. I think what happens is that the more you do something, the more familiar you become with it — with arranging, with writing, with putting things together. You just do it more easily, more confidently."

It's fascinating to wonder what the material that didn't make it onto *Love Over Gold* might have been. It was reported at the time that the road schedule was to rule out an early follow-up to *Love Over Gold*. There was no shortage of material (twenty songs were written, with only five used on the LP and two more on the EP). The original plan was for this album to be a double.

Knopfler was clearly overflowing with ideas: "I think it would be great to do another album soon. The only thing is that everybody wants us to go and play. It's simply a matter of time. If they really want you to go there, it's nice to go and say hello. So I've still got a bunch of tunes hanging around, if anybody wants some songs…"

Released on LP and cassette in September 1982, *Love Over Gold* is reported to have sold two million copies within the first six weeks of its release. It got to number one in not only the UK (where it stayed for four weeks), but in Australia, Austria, Italy, New Zealand and Norway. It got to number nineteen in the US. The album was later certified gold in the US, platinum in France and Germany and double-platinum in the UK and Canada.

The 1996 international remastered CD release of *Love Over Gold* features an alteration to the original cover art whereby the album title sits underneath the band's name — both in larger font — rather than arranged over the top. The image of the lightening is also more close-up. It is the only Dire Straits album where the cover art on the CD is altered in comparison to what was featured on the original LP release. The remastered version of the album released on CD in the US in 2000 retained the original cover art as it was on the LP.

It was asserted in *Melody Maker* in October 1982; "Dire Straits are band that catch you unawares. After the fun city jollity of their first album, a hook in every riff, a barb in every comment, they came up with the much-derided *Communiqué*. 'Romeo And Juliet' came off the wall, and so-called informed opinion gave 'Private Investigations' no chance. What do they know? 'Twisting By The Pool' will also catch some of you unawares, but in fact it's an old song. A one-time encore, it's a bootleggers' favourite and appeared in a BBC Two *Arena* documentary first shown a couple of years back, albeit in a rather deft fantasy sequence and now repeated tonight. Given that moody introspection has propelled both 'Private Investigations' and *Love Over Gold* to the top, it seemed an unusual choice."

Knopfler said, "It's ancient, but people have always been bugging me to do it. It rocks now, it swings. The end of it really came out of a development of the way we used to end

'News' onstage and I've been orchestrating it more, so it's really glued onto a tune that I just started playing. You learn more all the time. While I've been off the road I've been trying to get better. I think it's important to get better at what you do."

After quoting some lyrics from the title track ("It takes love over gold and mind over matter…"), *Sounds* reviewed *Love Over Gold* in October 1982; "Taken from this album's title track, these are the lyrics that Mark Knopfler has very purposefully had reprinted on all the music press ads for this hotly anticipated magnum opus — I can think of very few releases that I have awaited with such expectation as this one — and they represent a very clear declaration of intent as far as the overall content and feel of the album and its creator is concerned. *Love Over Gold* or artistic gratification for mercenary commercialism if you like, and there's no doubt that this fourth Dire Straits album marks a very significant maturation for Knopfler and his band, the first indications of which were apparent on the completely anti-tradition character of the current chart-topping single."

"For all those who felt happier convinced that Dire Straits were just a passing phenomenon who would continue doing production-line re-spray jobs on their lead guitarist's quirky style and gentle rock 'n' roll until they faded into the tax-haven sunset, this album comes as a resounding slap in the face. It's proof positive that Knopfler has both a bubbling, barely-tapped well of musical talent *and* the courage and determination to stretch and flex that talent to the full, with no regard for the constricting conventions of how "pop stars" are supposed to go about becoming successful salesmen of their marketable commodity. I read in a recent interview with guitarist Hal Lindes — who, along with Alan Clark on keyboards, makes his Straits vinyl debut with this album, which is ironically also drummer Pick Withers' swansong — that he thought 'Private Investigations' was 'off the wall' as a single and that the whole style and nature of the album was an overflow from the film-score work that Knopfler has recently been involved in."

"And with just five tracks filling both sides of this (classical vinyl-pressed) album — one of them is a mammoth epic of over fourteen minutes — this is indeed a long way from a regulation-style rock album, but far from slipping into obsessive over-indulgence. What Knopfler has done here is give room for his songs to grow and flower, free from the shackles of the standard verse-chorus-middle eight-outro syndrome. In conjunction with this musical expansiveness, the album is also the most impressive showcase to date for Knopfler's incredibly versatile guitar virtuosity, varying from semi-classical flamenco guitar picking of 'Private Investigations' to a scorching bluesy wah-wah solo at the coda of 'It Never Rains' with the kind of fiery passion that used to be the sole property of old Slowhand Clapton himself."

The review continued: "But to details: The elegiac 'Telegraph Road' kicks off the album with a silver thread of tinkling piano and gentle acoustic guitar broadening into a blazing sunburst of elaborate synth embroidery, rapid-fire drums and that familiar tingling Knopfler guitar sound, the tempo ebbing and flowing from wailing heights to tranquil lows and finally into a plectrum-smouldering climax. After that epic, the side is concluded by the now familiar ringing tones of 'Private Investigations' — only *two* tracks on a side! Not since the days of 'Inna-Gadda-Da-Vida'. Still, things get a shade more conventional on side two, with *three* tracks headed by 'Industrial Disease' — and for all of you who thought Knopfler's lyrics were invariably some elliptical and obscure parable of unrequited love or a decimated id, here's a song whose words are direct, humorous and with a very pointed and relevant social message to deliver."

"Throughout the album, Knopfler's voice sounds like a cross between the Dylan slur and the John Cooper Clarke speed-spiel, but particularly on this track as he twists his tongue around the whizzing verbals of the verses. And though the tune itself is fairly simple and repetitive, there are some really beautiful guitar touches at the end with

Knopfler just striking out those heavy chopped chords and leaving acres of space for your own imagination to fill in the backing details, demonstrating that the mark (no pun intended) of a true guitar virtuoso is often not what he plays, but the spaces he leaves in between the notes."

"On to the title track then and if Knopfler was the Sultan Of Swing on the last number, he's the Nabob Of Sob on this one, the album's only true romantic ballad — and very poignant it is too. Which brings us to the finale of 'It Never Rains', which is once again a deceptively simple, easy-swinging song that provides yet another intriguing insight into the psyche of this retiring "guitar hero" and ends in that awesome display of guitar fireworks on the wah-wah pedal. The commercial success of the album is already without doubt, with the advance sales giving it immediate gold status. But much more important, this represents the most adventurous and mesmeric Dire Straits album so far, borne high on the shoulders of Mark Knopfler's highly individual musical brilliance."

Rolling Stone reviewed *Love Over Gold* in November 1982; "*Love Over Gold* is not just the title of Dire Straits' fourth album, it is a statement of purpose. In almost suicidal defiance of commercial good sense, singer-songwriter-guitarist Mark Knopfler has chosen to follow his muse, fashioning a collection of radically expanded epics and evocative tone poems that demand the listener's undivided attention. Certainly a quantum leap from the organic R&B impressionism of the band's early LPs (*Dire Straits* and *Communiqué*) and the gripping short stories of *Making Movies*, its 1980 best seller, *Love Over Gold* is an ambitious, sometimes difficult record that is exhilarating in its successes and, at the very least, fascinating in its indulgences."

"Two drastically different moods dominate the new album. One is sharp and fiery (like the bolt of lightning on the cover); the other is soft and seductive. That dichotomy is particularly explicit in 'Private Investigations', a long, unorthodox ballad in which Knopfler plays a private detective hardened by a life of combing through other people's dirty laundry. Over a discreet synthesiser ring, gurgling marimba and a delicately plucked acoustic guitar, he grumbles into his whiskey glass like Bob Dylan in a trench coat: 'You get to meet all sorts...,' he recites in a raspy nicotine snarl. Then John Illsley sounds a quiet warning with a stalking bass line before the song erupts in dramatic bursts of guitar gunfire and tragic-sounding piano playing. This wracking schizophrenia between the heart and the heartless, the loving and the pain, has always informed Knopfler's songs and arrangements."

"*Love Over Gold*, however, finds Knopfler casting further than ever for ways to articulate the frustrations that colour his romantic streak. At nearly fifteen minutes, the album's opener, 'Telegraph Road', is certainly a challenge to the average pop fan's attention span. But the song's historic sweep and intimate tension — the building of America and the dashing of one man's dreams in the wake of its accelerating crumble — enable Knopfler to deploy a variety of surprising instrumental voices, from the synthesised sunrise whistle at the beginning to the baroque piano motif in the middle. The song closes with an extended solo guitar crescendo that's heated up by Pick Withers' galloping drums. 'Love Over Gold' is a whispery ballad that plays the jazzy tingle of vibes against an almost classical piano air and the violin-like pluck of a synthesiser to heighten its images of a casual, even cavalier, sex life."

"On the other hand, 'Industrial Disease' — at five minutes, the shortest of the LP's five songs and its most conventional rocker — crackles with a cynicism underlined by its cheesy 'Wooly Bully' organ and coughing guitar effect. At times, Mark Knopfler, who also plays producer here, seems to try too hard. 'It Never Rains' is a harsh chip off the 'Like A Rolling Stone' block. And nearly all the songs end in guitar solos, as if he had too many ideas and was unsure how to reconcile them. But in a period when most pop music

Prince Charles is privileged to meet the band backstage at the Dominion Theatre, London, where they were performing in the Prince's Trust rock gala charity concert on 20th July 1983.

The five-man line-up.
Left to right: Terry Williams, Alan Clark, Mark Knopfler, Hal Lindes, John Illsley.

is conceived purely as product, *Love Over Gold* dares to put art before airplay." (The "art over airplay" comment though; what a complement for any artist to have it recognised — or at least considered — that their output was done with the intention of creating something innovative rather than going straight for the commercial jugular as it were).

In January 1983, *Love Over Gold* was reviewed in *The University of Wisconsin Pointer*; "This band has come a long way since their debut album *Dire Straits* won critic's choice and immediate popular success. The release of *Love Over Gold* puts this band in the spotlight of musical maturity... Fourteen and a half minutes of 'Telegraph Road' give an historical account of industry and the profit motive. And every time 'Industrial Disease' comes on, all that comes to mind is all the aldicarb junkies around the Portage County potato farms. Enough about subject matter. The music alone on the album makes *Love Over Gold* a Dire Straits classic, a must purchase for any fan, fresh or weathered. The addition of keyboard player Alan Clark has transformed the group from a great guitar band to a great band, period. Hal Lindes on guitar is another newcomer to the trio of Knopfler, explosive Pick Withers on drums, and perfectly unobtrusive John Illsley on bass. The bittersweet 'It Never Rains' is a song to be reckoned with. Use caution when being captured by the hypnotic out music. Repeated play may warrant repeated play."

Upon being asked if after *Love Over Gold*, was there a feeling that there needed to be some commercial singles on the next album, Alan Clark was quoted in *Ultimate Classic Rock* in May 2014; "No. Not even a tiny little bit. If there ever was, Mark would have dispelled it immediately. There was no record company pressure whatsoever. I think maybe on the second record, *Communiqué*, he might have felt that pressure, but then he was new to the game and went along with it and realised his mistake very early on of trying to recreate the first record. So after that, there was no pressure whatsoever."

It was considered in *Rolling Stone* in January 1983; "Knopfler's determination to mould Dire Straits entirely in his own image has paid off in a 1983 group that's far more full-bodied and stylistically varied than the original foursome. Illsley remains on bass — an inventive player with the rangy good looks of a "real" rock star; American guitarist Hal Lindes ably punctuates Knopfler's leads; Alan Clark, once a sideman with Lindisfarne, and Tommy Mandel, another American, late of Ian Hunter's band, complement each other on keyboards; and the formidable Terry Williams — king of the straight 4/4 with Rockpile — recently slid into the drum seat. This latest edition of Dire Straits assembled one drizzly November night at the Woodwharf, a damp, dockside rehearsal facility on the Thames River. With Williams pumping on drums and the twin keyboards rising majestically over Knopfler's moody guitar figures, the group was kicking with new energy." To which Knopfler was quoted, "That band is steaming. There was smoke and flames coming out of that place." Illsley was quoted: "This is the happiest this band's ever been."

Although Dire Straits won Best British Group at the 1983 Brit Awards, staying humble probably helped to keep the band grounded. Knopfler was quoted in *Rolling Stone* in January 1983; "It makes me a little wary when people start saying, 'This is a work of genius,' or 'This is a masterpiece.' That's a kind of labelling too: 'Oh, yes, well, he does some masterpieces.' I'm just as happy doing a Phil Everly session, or playing 'Move It' or 'Sweet Little Rock And Roller'."

The *Love Over Gold* tour lasted eight months. During the tour, session keyboard player Tommy Mandel was brought in to the live line-up to help Clark get across the complexity of his keyboard parts on stage. The final dates of the tour were two sold-out shows at the Hammersmith Odeon on 22nd and 23rd July 1983. The double album, *Alchemy: Dire Straits Live*, features recordings that were made of those shows. It is reported to have been released without the addition of studio overdubs. Mixed in November 1983 and released in March 1984, it got to number three in the UK. Footage from the Hammersmith Odeon performances was also released on video. The material was later remastered and released on DVD and Blueray in 2010.

In January 1983, *Sounds* reported on a performance that took place at Wembley Arena; "If *Love Over Gold* was the zenith of Dire Straits' recording career to date, then their stage act represents the addition of several dimensions, each of which serves to embellish the subdued beauty of the album and establish the brilliance of Knopfler's visions. The atmosphere could not have been anything but vital — the album material was aired in its entirety, interspersed with gems from earlier offerings such as 'Once Upon A Time In The West' from the largely disappointing *Communiqué* and the delicious honky tonk of 'Sultans Of Swing' from the outstanding debut album."

"Also interesting was the inclusion of two new rockers, 'Twisting By The Pool' and 'Two Young Lovers' from a forthcoming EP, which show just how effectively the band can switch from the breathtaking and captivating to the homage-paying but nonetheless original forms of rock and roll. Two tracks which most befitted from a live situation — strangely, both from *Love Over Gold* — were 'Industrial Disease' and 'Telegraph Road'. The former, with Knopfler's filtered guitar sound chopping out chunks of rhythm against a melodramatic synth backdrop, was a sudden change from the ethereal 'Once Upon A Time In The West' which immediately preceded it while 'Industrial Disease' is a work of Springsteenesque domesticity and accordingly its effect, though initially specific, has a universal relevance. 'Telegraph Road', whether intentionally or not, takes on the Boss and beats him at his own game. It's an intense chronicle of the pioneer's elation, then frustration, then disillusionment — and with the presence of an audience from which Knopfler drew an invisible energy, the tale was more poignant than it is on record, his vocals (which can sound a mite too scratchy on vinyl) adding a bitter but necessary edge to the song's message. It is without doubt the epic which stands a proud head above the rest — which isn't a condemnation of the other material at all — but live, it reaches masterpiece levels."

"Similarly, 'Private Investigations' comes over with an intriguing vengeance. The cross-spotlighting during the half-whispered/half-crooned lyrics emphasised the bleakness and the solitude of the moment and the thickly stagnant dry ice said as much about the situation as the words did. The crescendo into the crashing chords was superbly controlled by the other guitarist Hal Lindes, who complemented Knopfler's playing throughout the set and provided an essential foil to his sweet guitar melodies. During the introduction to 'Sultans Of Swing', the two girls in front of me decided they had sat for long enough and that the time had come to dance. Up they popped and bang went my clear view of the stage, but the music was speaking for itself — a joyous tribute to itself. Not self-centred, not introverted, but instead, celebratory and unrestrained."

There was so much going on for Dire Straits that everything was probably rushing past them at the speed of light. Mark Knopfler was quoted in *Rolling Stone* in January 1983; "I often find that success is perceived much more by people outside than by the people who're involved in it. The people who're involved in it are usually so bloody busy that they don't have time to think about it at all."

Throughout 1983 and 1984, Mark Knopfler was active with other projects away from Dire Straits. As well as writing the music for the films *Local Hero* (on which Alan Clark contributed keyboards and Terry Williams contributed drums) and *Cal*, he produced Bob Dylan's *Infidels* album as well as producing on Aztec Camera's *Knife*. 'Going Home' (from *Local Hero*) is still played at St James' Park prior to the start of every Newcastle United match. In 1984, John Illsley released his first solo album, *Never Told A Soul*. Mark Knopfler and Terry Williams contributed as musicians.

Knopfler told *Melody Maker* in October 1982; "I'd play with anybody if they ask. I always get really excited about sessions." Regarding Mr Dylan, Knopfler — humble in his approach — was quoted in *Rolling Stone* in January 1983; "I love Bob. He's different in the sense that he didn't necessarily take to an instrument; he's much more a poet and writer — to him, that's all. Whereas I've just got this thing where I can strum a couple of chords."

Rolling Stone commented in January 1983; "Knopfler may in fact be the most lyrical rock guitarist since Jimi Hendrix died and Jeff Beck gave up the game. He is also, as the leader of England's Dire Straits, a serious songwriter. In this regard, he sometimes sounds uncannily like Dylan, and at other times — when he's talking about how he's 'run every red light on memory lane' — like Bruce Springsteen. But when Knopfler picks up a guitar, he speaks with his true voice — snarling on the bass strings, soaring up to nail a high, blue note, then fluttering away like a flurry of startled birds over the edges of the music. Although he seems immune to his own magic, he's something of a master himself."

On the difference between doing film music and working with Dire Straits, Knopfler explained to *Melody Maker* in October 1982; "You're doing it for somebody else. It's not such a personal deal. It's good for you because they might turn around and say 'Well, I don't like that' and you think 'Oh!' It's not usual for anyone in the band to say they don't like something. I think it's really good training and I'd like to do it again but I'm not sure whether I can do it. I think you have to do a few before you really get into the swing of it… You can bring in all different sides of yourself and bits of music that you've picked up and bring it all together. You have to use your imagination a lot. And sometimes you have to dig fairly deep."

Who are you looking at?

© Laurens van Houten / Pictorial Press Ltd / Alamy Stock Photo

John on stage at Hammersmith.

Brothers In Arms

In late 1984, Dire Straits took to recording some tracks at Air Studios in Montserrat. With Mark Knopfler and Neil Dorfsman producing, the sessions would see further personnel changes to the band. Due to Tommy Mandel going back to do session work, Guy Fletcher was brought in as a second keyboard player. Fletcher had previously worked with Steve Harley & Cockney Rebel, Roxy Music and Aztec Camera as well as on the *Cal* soundtrack. During the sessions for what would become *Brothers In Arms*, Hal Lindes left and was replaced by Jack Sonni, a guitar player from New York. (Upon being asked whether or not he was in the habit of asking other members of the band for advice on lyrics, Knopfler was quoted in *Rolling Stone* in November 1985; "No, never have. I can only recall one time, with one word: Jack (Sonni) suggested I use makeup in 'Money For Nothing' instead of tutu. I was using tutu.")

It was during the recording sessions for *Brothers In Arms* that Dorfsman considered drummer Terry Williams no longer suitable for the sound that Dire Straits were aiming to create. As a result, jazz session drummer Omar Hakim was brought in to re-record the drum parts. He did the whole thing in two days and then left to fulfil other commitments. Although both Williams and Hakim are credited on the album, the only work of Williams' that made it to the final cut was the improvised cadenza on the opening of 'Money For Nothing'.

Dorfsman said in *Sound On Sound* in May 2006; "Having done the rhythm track, we therefore decided to make an extended intro with Terry. We all felt this was definitely his style, so we set up his five toms and snare and did that as a separate piece. Guy laid down a guide keyboard and we just kind of conducted Terry, urging him to get wilder and wilder as the intro went on. That was already in place by the time Omar came in and we all really loved it, so then it was basically just a case of getting the drum track."

"I'd always had my doubts that we were getting what we needed on the rhythm tracks, and I remember telling Mark early on that the drums weren't really happening. Initially, he didn't feel the same way, but after several weeks he picked up on my frustration. So, we decided to ditch the drums and bring in a new drummer to overdub onto the existing tracks. I remember Mark talking about maybe getting Roxy Music's Andy Newmark or the jazz drummer Peter Erskine, but eventually we sent for Omar Hakim. On the New York scene he was known more as a jazz-fusion drummer than as a rock drummer, but he was the kind of guy who could play anything and Mark was a big fan of his, so we brought him down to Montserrat and he re-did all of the tracks in about two and a half days. The first day he did about six, the next day he did three or four, and he was out of there by the third day. That was pretty mind-blowing."

"The difference, once he played, was night and day. It really started to sound like a record. Omar is very, very confident as a musician and as a person, and what he brought to it was exactly what it needed, which was kind of a kick in the butt. Beforehand, it wasn't so much a comfort zone in the studio as it was an over-relaxed zone — we were there in Montserrat, it was beautiful, there was a lot of swimming, a lot of hanging out, and basically we got into a thing where the energy slowly, slowly, slowly ebbed away. It was like being on a vacation for a while and losing a little bit of edge without even realising it. The music needed that energy and we weren't really getting it. We weren't vibing at all, but then I remember Omar coming in and it was like a bulldozer — New York attitude, New York energy."

"He sat behind the kit, we did a run-through of 'So Far Away' — which ended up being the first song on the record — and it was just amazing. Not that he played anything so incredibly inventive, but it was just so right in terms of his vibe, his sound and his energy. We knew right away, and it continued from there. I think he did three takes of that song, three or four takes of each tune after that, and there was no compiling or even punching in. Omar listened to the tunes and they already had drums on there, so he knew what the parts would be, and then he just got on with the job. I mean, he brought his own feel to the material; a little bit more energy, a little bit more complicated playing, and I think it quite literally saved the project."

On the specific differences between Terry Williams' and Omar Hakim's drumming styles, Dorfsman said; "To me, the record was sounding more like a demo, and this really hit home when we tried to do the song 'Ride Across The River'. It was laying there like lead. I don't think Terry felt that rhythm, and that was totally understandable. Having played with Dave Edmunds and Rockpile, that wasn't what he was famous for. He was a great drummer, but his style was more straight-ahead rock and roll, whereas Omar's style was more polyrhythmic and better suited to the direction in which Mark was going. The material needed the kind of glossy sheen that Omar brought, as well as his versatility — there was a lot of different music on the record: 'Your Latest Trick' was kind of jazzy and 'Ride Across The River' had that reggae-ish feel, so we needed a drummer who was versed in a lot of different styles and Omar fit the bill in that regard. Believe me, it was a load off my mind when he played that first tune and knocked everybody out. It was a big deal to fly somebody in from New York, not really knowing one hundred percent if things would go according to plan. I had worked with him a bunch in the past and knew he was great, but I still didn't really know if he was going to be the right guy for the job. Thank God, for that particular record, the right call was made. There were definitely some sweaty moments."

Although Andy Kanavan briefly played drums, Williams would remain a member of Dire Straits for the music videos and the *Brothers In Arms* world tour thereafter. In response to the question of "There have been a lot of personnel changes in the band, and one hears you're a stern taskmaster. Do you think you are?" Knopfler responded; "No. That's one of the things you can't win. If you are, you're a dictator. If you're not, you're a wimp. Ninety-five percent of the time I like being the fearless leader. I just think that when you write a song and get it together, you want to get it done right.

Now if that sometimes involves making people work long hours in rehearsals, that's fair enough. Sometimes, I make the mistake of stopping and waiting for somebody else to give, waiting for somebody else to show how much they care. I've done that a few times, and I don't think it gets you very far."

Regarding Dorfsman, Knopfler said in *Musician* in September 1985; "Neil's always had a lot of input, but he's developed more and more, he's become a more experienced record maker. If anything, I would say that I wrote the songs and helped organise the music and Neil produced this record."

In response to the question of "how had the band changed and evolved by the time you went back into the studio to start working on what would become the *Brothers In Arms* album?" Alan Clark said in 2014; "I think after *Love Over Gold*, because it was heavily keyboard oriented, Mark doesn't like to stand still and the reason for that is largely because when he made the very first Dire Straits record and the *Communiqué* record, he realised that the producers were trying to recreate the first record and that was a lesson he obviously learned and one that he vowed he would never repeat. So every record that Mark made with Dire Straits was different to the previous one and quite rightfully so. We made a conscious decision to not include much piano for instance, which worked out fine because we ended up recording the record in Montserrat in the Caribbean and the piano there wasn't great anyway. So that's one of the reasons why there wasn't a great deal of piano on that record, actually. He decided to write a bunch of stuff in a different area really, which worked out very well, actually."

The release of *Brothers In Arms* was an achievement in and of itself. A faulty batch of recording tape had resulted in three tracks being lost. It delayed things by around a week or so — time that could little afford to be wasted considering that the band had to finish the album in time for the tour. Neil Dorfsman recalled in *Sound On Sound* in May 2006; "I actually didn't expect the record to do what it did. I knew the band was very popular, but no one ever thought the album would turn out to be so huge."

Brothers In Arms was released in May 1985. It got to number one in the UK where it spent a total of two hundred and twenty-eight weeks in the charts. It sold over 4.3 million copies and went on to become the UK's bestselling album in the year of its release. The album had stratospheric success in the US whereby it stayed in the number one spot for nine weeks. It sold nine million copies and went multi-platinum. It also stayed in Australia's number one spot for thirty-four weeks. No other album has held the same record to this day. *The New York Times* reported in September 1985 that *Brothers In Arms* "may be the finest mainstream rock record of 1985. The album, which soared to number one on Billboard's pop album chart two weeks ago, has already sold nearly two million copies and has spawned one of the year's most controversial hits in 'Money For Nothing' (number six on Billboard's singles chart and climbing rapidly)."

Rolling Stone reviewed *Brothers In Arms* in July 1985; "Except for their swell debut hit single, 'Sultans Of Swing', in 1979, the British band Dire Straits has never come as much of a surprise. And, then, what caught you off guard was how much the singer sounded like Dylan. *Brothers In Arms*, their first studio album since *Love Over Gold* three years ago, offers more of their winsomely rocking tunes. The band is augmented by bassist Tony Levin, Weather Report drummer Omar Hakim, a horn section, which includes the Brecker Brothers, and some thirteen different keyboards that are used to explore orchestral textures."

"Carefully crafted instead of raucous, pretty rather than booming, and occasionally affecting, the record is beautifully produced, with Mark Knopfler's terrific guitar work catching the best light. The lyrics are literate, but the scenarios aren't as interesting as they used to be on records like *Making Movies*, still the band's most solid LP. Side one has the most driving songs: the bouncy 'Walk Of Life', a fifties rock and roll song about cool fifties rock and roll songs that features a cheesy organ sound, and 'So Far Away', a missive from a distant town, with a catchy bass line rumbling underneath it."

"After a grandiose introduction, 'Money For Nothing' shows what a guy who moves refrigerators for a living thinks of the rock stars on MTV. 'See the little faggot… he's a millionaire,' the guy mutters, while Knopfler's guitar grinds out his irritation. The guitar turns delicate for the gentle 'Why Worry', a song that's as soft as a sigh. Side two, made up of four songs about men and war, is more ambitious and less successful. Knopfler practically whispers the lyric to 'Brothers In Arms' but never turns out images that catch your eye; the music's lovely, though, with the electric guitar cutting patterns in a soft-toned background. But no telling metaphors are found in this quartet of songs, and the music lacks the ache that made Knopfler's recent soundtracks for *Comfort And Joy* and *Cal* so powerful."

Despite the way in which *Brothers In Arms* has generally gone down in history as a strong album — not just for Dire Straits but overall — when it was new to the world, the occasional scathing review was not non-existent. Under the heading of "Dire Straits — Stuck In A Forgettable Groove", *The Los Angeles Times* reviewed the album in May 1985; "This English band came along in 1978 with a subdued country-blues sound that was the antithesis of the punk and new wave which was then the rage. Mark Knopfler's supple, subtle guitar style and softly Dylanesque voice were a welcome contrast to prevailing rock for those who were less than happy about the Sex Pistols' assault on pop sensibilities. The trouble with Dire Straits is that its sound seemed caught up in a whirlpool. Though it enjoys considerable international popularity, the band has stuck to pretty much the same game plan since the initial 'Sultans Of Swing'. Knopfler may be a guitar whiz and his soundtrack LPs are enchanting mood pieces, but the second Dire Straits album sounded pretty much like the first, and so on. You'd think that the passing of two and a half years since the last studio LP, *Love Over Gold*, might lead to some new wrinkles. Think again. Like all Dire Straits recordings, *Brothers In Arms* is easy to listen to, but unmemorable."

"On top of that, Knopfler's writing has lost much of its edge. 'Money For Nothing', a wry, envious look at rock stardom, is almost worthy of Randy Newman, but it's not worth seven minutes and four seconds. 'Ride Across The River' is an ordinary anti-war statement that would have seemed a long ride at three minutes. At more than twice that length, it's like an ocean voyage on an ill-equipped raft. The band seems bored on this and other shuffling tunes like 'So Far Away' and 'Walk Of Life', and boredom is contagious. Of the long songs, only the slowest, the title track, justifies its length. The most successful tracks, generally, are the ones that come closest to rocking the sprightly blues 'One World' and the John Wesley Harding-like outlaw-folk workout, 'The Man's Too Strong'. These are the closest tranquil Knopfler comes to extremes, and he's best heard at those extremes: either tranquil or dynamic. Unfortunately, most of this album falls somewhere in the dull, stagnant middle."

With the advantage of hindsight, it would be easy to assume that *Brothers In Arms* was strongly supported by the music press but in reality, this wasn't the case. The album was reviewed in *Melody Maker* in May 1985; "It says right here that *Brothers In Arms* signals the official end of a two year period of hibernation by Mark Knopfler and the rest of the Dire Straits. Clearly, the original Sultan of Swing has a rather odd attitude to resting up, using this supposed break from the platinum trail to get involved in all manner of things, most notably film, Dylan and young Roddy Frame. Unfortunately for the rest of us, this admirable spirit of adventure fails to materialise when it comes to *Brothers In Arms*. Instead, it all sounds a bit too like the last Dire Straits album, which sounded not unlike the last one before that, which sounded suspiciously like the beginning of a hugely successful and very lucrative plan to take over the world known as AOR."

"And as with all such mega-dollar scams, the basic idea is remarkably simple. World-weary, almost whisky-soaked vocals, a guitar sound designed purely for digital recording, and lots more songs about TV and girls. Highlights? Ah, possibly 'Why Worry', a typical Knopfler ballad-cum-*Tales Of The Riverbank* arrangement, and most certainly the title track, which manages to overshadow everything else on display, showing off the major new lessons in atmospherics and dynamics that must have been learnt on the recent *Cal/Local Hero* soundtracks. Talking of which, Mark Knopfler will now undoubtedly go on to much greater things, arranging and producing work for a whole host of artists, and generally establishing himself as the nearest thing we yet have to a very English and much thinner Vangelis. When it comes to Dire Straits however, the old rock-school restraints and undeniably attractive smell of the winning formula seem to block out any such experimental work and what you end up with is something very like the same old story."

Of course, there was no lack of glowing reviews as well. *International Musician And Recording World* commented in January 1986; "*Brothers In Arms* is generally regarded as Dire Straits' best-sounding album to date. It runs the gamut, from standard Straits' power twangers ('Money For Nothing', 'The Man's Too Strong') to lilting opuses such as 'Why Worry' and 'So Far Away', to keyboard/guitar exercises like the title track. Of course, there's plenty of Knopfler's undeniable unfashionability — numerous six and seven minute songs in this era of three-minute pop packages. Throughout his career Knopfler — a one-time schoolteacher and a rock critic for the *Yorkshire Evening Post* — has defied convention and avoided the pop star wagon train."

Brothers In Arms is listed in the *Guinness Book of World Records* as the first album released on CD to sell a million copies. Many consider the album to have been pivotal in popularising the CD format. The CD release of *Brothers In Arms* featured the full version of 'Money For Nothing' in comparison to the version on the LP. The CD release of the album also boasts extended versions of all tracks on the first side of the LP (with 'Walk Of Life' being the exception). 'Brothers In Arms' was one of the first singles to be released on CD format. In the UK, it was issued as a promotional piece for the Dire Straits' tour, Live in '85. 'Money For Nothing' got to number four in the UK and to number one in the US. It was awarded a Grammy for Best Rock Performance By A Duo Or Group With Vocal in February 1986.

1986 saw Dire Straits awarded two Grammys. In 1987 they were awarded Best British Album at the Brits. As of December 2017, *Brothers In Arms* has been ranked as the eighth-best-selling album in UK chart history. Compared to Dire Straits' previous albums, *Brothers In Arms* had a more elaborate production. It was the first album to be recorded entirely digitally due to Mark Knopfler feeling strongly that the opportunity for improved sound quality should be embraced.

The Ottawa Citizen wrote in May 1985; "If then bassist John Illsley put out a solo album last year, some wondered whether anything more would come of Dire Straits. Band leader Mark Knopfler had been juggling numerous extracurricular projects, including soundtracks and work with Tina Turner, Bob Dylan, Aztec Camera among others. Meanwhile, the band had not put out a studio album since *Love Over Gold* in 1982. Now these side bars appear to have served a purpose. The excursions have helped the band extend its scope."

"That process had begun with the EP 'Twisting By The Pool', an exercise in garage rock and roll which was the polar opposite of the carefully studied musicianship of *Love Over Gold*. It continues with the addition of ex-Weather Report drummer Omar Hakim and a full horn section that includes the Brecker Brothers, all of whom also bring new factors into the equation. *Brothers In Arms* is a diverse album reflecting this input which is expertly sequenced so that each turn flows seamlessly. This is not a simple chore considering the range of moods which stretch from big beat songs about the dangers of recoiling into a rock and roll fantasy to the sombre confessions of a war criminal. Songs like 'Walk Of Life' with its farfisa-like organ riff seem to be extensions of 'Twisting By The Pool'. It refers to vintage rock and roll without attempting to revive it, something few outside of Bruce Springsteen are capable of doing."

"Other tracks embrace a jazz influence. 'Your Latest Trick', however, which is dominated by percussion and horns comes as close as Dire Straits could or should get to Chuck Mangione. In general, though, the band is not in such an amiable mood. With 'Money For Nothing', it levels a scathing attack on MTV and all of the rock junk culture associated with, or symbolised by, the video racket. The most emotionally intense songs are those centred on themes of war and religion. While Mark Knopfler's guitarwork, with its trail of soft, mournful notes, is the element linking all of this material, it is here that it is the most poignant. Among these tracks is 'Brothers In Arms' which tries to make sense out of the 'fields of destruction' and the 'baptism of fire'. It is somehow appropriate that the massive one year, twenty-five country global trek the band is undertaking in support of *Brothers In Arms* began in Jerusalem. Like Bob Dylan's *Infidels*, on which Knopfler also worked, the Middle East is a metaphoric point of departure where everything begins and ends."

Notably, it seems that the journalist of the above perhaps missed the intention of irony behind 'Money For Nothing'. If they did, they certainly weren't the only ones to do so. *The New York Times* reported in September 1985; "Inevitably, the irony of the song has sailed over some people's heads, including some reviewers, and there have been complaints in the homosexual press that the song condones the use of bigoted language."

Knopfler retorted, "The same thing happened when Randy Newman recorded 'Short People', a song that was clearly about the stupidity of prejudice. An editor of *Gay News* in England attacked the song. What surprises me is that an intelligent journalist can misunderstand it."

Mark Knopfler was well aware of the extents to which the irony in 'Money For Nothing' seemed to be lost on some people. He was quoted in *Rolling Stone* in November 1985; "I got an objection from the editor of a gay newspaper in London — he actually said it was 'below the belt'. Apart from the fact that there are stupid gay people as well as stupid other people, it suggests that maybe you can't let it have so many meanings — you have to be direct. In fact, I'm still of two minds as to whether it's a good idea to write songs that aren't in the first person, to take on other characters. The singer in 'Money For Nothing' is a real ignoramus, hardhat mentality — somebody who sees everything in financial terms. I mean, this guy has a grudging respect for rock stars. He sees it in terms of, well, that's not working and yet the guy's rich; that's a good scam. He isn't sneering."

The New York Times reported in September 1985; "'Money For Nothing' is a pungent dramatic monologue in which a swaggering appliance store clerk banters with his colleagues about MTV. The lyric begins: 'Now look at them yo-yo's...'. In the second verse, the speaker directs his scorn at pretty-boy pop stars. Using an offensive epithet for homosexuals to describe a singer who wears a gold earring and makeup, he speculates that the star is a millionaire with his own jet airplane. Written and performed by Mark Knopfler, Dire Straits' Scottish-born lead singer, songwriter, lead guitarist and co-producer, 'Money For Nothing' is the first major hit to take aim at worship of rock-video stars and the envy and resentment that are the inevitable backwash of such adulation. The song acknowledges one of the most disturbing aspects of music-videos: the fact that by watching performers lip-synch to their own records, it is possible for an audience to entertain the illusion that the musicians don't really work, since the job of making music is reduced to mere posing. The song owes its immediacy to the fact that its offensive language — deleted for top forty radio air play — was taken from dialogue that Mr

Knopfler actually overheard."

Knopfler explained, "I was in an appliance store on the Upper East Side in which all the TV sets were tuned to MTV. A couple of guys who worked there were discoursing on the acts that were appearing... I went to the front of the store and asked for a piece of paper so I could write down what they were saying, because I was intrigued by their notion that these musicians were impossibly rich without actually having to work."

He told *Musician* in September 1985; "I wanted to use the language the guy really used. It was more real. I did use 'that little faggot,' but there were a couple of good 'mother-fuckers' — which mean nothing to you in a hardware store in New York City, but which might mean something to people who live in Tallahassee. There's no way I could expect people to receive that in the spirit it's intended. They'd probably think I was just being vulgar. Still, if we have time, I might record a version with the real language, just to have it for myself."

And in *International Musician And Recording World* in January 1986; "There's only one way to get someone to understand all that goes into this gig, and that would be not to just have him come to the show, but to have him come to soundcheck every day, have him stay with me all the time. Even then he would have no concept of what it means to go through months of recording, months of rehearsals, hundreds of hours of writing, dealing with a band, organising a tour, doing videos, doing interviews — it's such a long cycle, so much is involved in this thing. Even so, I didn't hate that guy in the store just because he was a prejudiced blockhead; I loved him even though he represented everything I can't stand."

Sting contributed guest vocals to 'Money For Nothing' and also shares a co-writing credit on it with Mark Knopfler. It was the use of the melody from 'Don't Stand So Close To Me' that resulted in Sting being given a writing credit. Notably, he didn't write any lyrics or indeed other parts of the song. Knopfler said in 2019; "I'd seen The Police doing an MTV advert, saying 'I want my MTV', just saying it all together; and I thought, 'If I set that to the notes of 'Don't Stand So Close To Me' it'll work.' I remember saying to the guys, 'I'd really like to get Sting to do this.' We knew them anyway because we'd done a lot of gigs together in Germany. One of them said, 'That's fine, because he's here on holiday.' And because I'd used the five notes from 'Don't Stand So Close To Me', that's how the co-writing thing happened, which is fine; it's absolutely fine with me and it worked out well. I remember quite clearly Sting coming into the studio and saying, 'What's wrong?' I said, 'What do you mean?' He said, 'Nobody's fighting!'"

Neil Dorfsman recalled; "Mark was a very casual vocalist. He'd often be smoking a cigarette while he sang, and we'd probably do six or seven similar passes and I would put something together. I'd always compile the vocals. That was something I took pride in. And it was while Sting was visiting Montserrat on vacation, having already recorded there with The Police, that Mark asked him to sing on 'Money For Nothing', lifting the tune from 'Don't Stand So Close To Me'. I knew Mark had already written the line 'I want my MTV', but I wasn't sure if he had the melody of 'Don't Stand So Close To Me' in mind. It was one of those things where Sting just sort of did it in three passes, I comped the thing, and then I walked around thinking 'There's something amazing about this.' It was done in about an hour... It was pretty mind-blowing, because I didn't expect anything. I just finished the record and moved on, thinking it would be a fairly successful Dire Straits record because they had a huge fan base. But it turned out to be something else."

August 1986 marked the launch of MTV in Europe. The 'Money For Nothing' video was the first to be played. British filmmaker Steve Barron directed the video. He had already made a name for himself having directed the video for Michael Jackson's 'Billie Jean' in early 1983. In 1985, Barron was approached by an executive from Warner Brothers, Jeff Ayeroff, who persuaded him to fly out to Budapest to ask Dire Straits, then on tour, if they'd like to do a video with him. Barron discussed the prospect with Knopfler over dinner but apparently, the guitarist didn't seem overly enthusiastic.

As Barron recalled in his 2014 book, *Egg n Chips & Billie Jean: A Trip Through The Eighties*; "I never did hear a yes. Nor an okay. Or a let's go for it. But there wasn't a no. Or a never. Or anything that said we couldn't. We'll just do it and pray that our Bosch FGS4000 delivers the goods." (the Bosch FGS4000 — also known as the Paintbox — was the computer workstation used to make the whole video for 'Money For Nothing'). The video made liberal use of CGI (Computer-Generated Imagery).

Barron, along with Ian Pearson as the computer graphics expert on the project, was given full director's control over the video. Advantageous as that may have been for them, dealing with the technology in its infancy was such that Pearson had to spend three and a half weeks living in the studio in order to get the video finished on time.

Regarding the 'Money For Nothing' video and what he would have preferred it to be, Mark Knopfler recalled in 2019; "To me it was almost like a dream sequence. I'd visualised a kid in his bedroom with that 'I want my MTV' thing happening and the camera rushing over the landscape — as I've said before, it's a good thing I never had anything to do with the video!"

In *Rolling Stone* in November 1985, the interviewer asked: "Your songwriting has undergone a major shift in recent years, from the evocative, atmospheric quality of 'Wild West End' and 'Down To The Waterline' to the simpler, more direct verse on *Brothers In Arms*. What inspired that change?" Knopfler replied: "I'm not saying I've had it with ambiguity or that things can't be multilayered. I've just become more drawn to writing those kinds of songs, where there is no problem in terms of who's singing what. If I listen to Willie Nelson sing 'Blue Skies', it always strikes me as great, very simple and direct. Sometimes it's better to go for the big, broad, beautiful statement rather than start getting involved in all this ambiguity. I think 'Born In The USA' is a classic example. Even Reagan can come in and invoke the spirit of Springsteen and couple him with Rambo. Bruce is trying to say, I think, that there's absolutely nothing wrong with loving your country, and there's nothing wrong with good citizenship. But the meaning has been taken and distorted by outsiders and used for their own purposes. I certainly don't want Reagan coming on to my songs and using them. I'd certainly have something to say to him about it if he tried, too."

On balancing his approach to writing, Knopfler told *Musician* in September 1985; "It's always based on music you like to play. It's a weird business. It has to have a whole harmonic balance. You try to create something that will work on a number of levels — it's functional, it's beautiful, it makes a point, it has its own reality. I'm not saying that everything is a crisis, but everywhere there are choices. You try staying outside while being inside, too. You can't just enter into the depths of the thing and have bits of paint flying all over the place. It's also important to stand back and look at what you're painting."

The New York Times commented in September 1985; "Fictional characters through whom Mr Knopfler contemplates masculine aggression include a Rudolf Hess-like war criminal in 'The Man's Too Strong', and two characters who blend into one — a soldier of freedom and a soldier of fortune — in 'Ride Across The River'. Mr Knopfler has framed these characters in cinematically detailed musical settings complete with horn fanfares and orchestrally rich keyboard textures. While the messages of the lyrics emerge as strongly pacifist, the music dramatises the romantic allure of combat and hierarchical command. And the interplay of Mr Knopfler's sullen growl of a voice — a gentler Celtic echo of Bob Dylan — with his brooding lyrical guitar solos underscores the tension, and often the deliberate confusion, in his songs between the heroic and the demonic aspects of comradeship."

Regarding 'The Man's Too Strong', Mark said in *Musician* in September 1985; "It's a study in guilt, hatred and fear. It could be a Hess-like figure in the depths of Spandau Prison, or anybody who's not at peace with himself... On 'The Man's Too Strong' I was just trying to get into the mind of somebody who's lived his life that way. It's an experiment in character, in play-writing I suppose."

The album's title track was written during Britain's engagement in the Falklands War in 1982. The song explored the futility of war. When 2007 marked the twenty fifth anniversary of the war, Mark Knopfler recorded a new version of the song at Abbey Road Studios. He did it to raise funds for the British veterans who he keenly acknowledged were still suffering from their experiences of the war. Poignantly, 'Brothers In Arms' has become a popular choice to play at military funerals.

Knopfler said in *Musician* in September 1985; "'Brothers In Arms' is written from the point of view of a soldier dying on the battlefield. To write something like that you can't just write off the top of your head. You have to dig deep if the thing's going to be realistic. You're an outsider, but to do it properly you're also digging inside. I don't think you can get away scot-free. If you do the song's not going to work. The whole area of creation plays all kinds of tricks on the writer. It can fool him into thinking it's easier than it is; it can fool him into thinking it's harder than it is; it can fool him into thinking it's working when it's not; or not working when it is."

The New York Times commented in September 1985; "'Money For Nothing' is only one of several songs on an album to explore ideas about brotherhood, machismo and soldiering from multiple perspectives."

Knopfler replied, "These issues are worth addressing, because there's such a potential for evil and destruction in all of us. I was inspired partly by William Broyles' article in *Esquire*, 'Why Men Love War'. It is the most intelligent and insidious rendering of the *Rambo* syndrome I've seen. As a kid, I used to love to play war games and go creeping around in the bushes."

He told *International Musician And Recording World* in January 1986; "I think if you look at the song 'Brothers In Arms', it has good depth, good melody and good orchestration. But then if you look at songs like 'Walk Of Life', they are in many ways throwbacks to the way our music's always been. The thing about *Brothers In Arms* is its range of music as opposed to its being more orchestrated. I wouldn't say it's more orchestrated than *Love Over Gold*, though there is some of that in there."

'Walk Of Life' got to number two in the UK and to number seven in the US. 'So Far Away' got to number twenty in the UK and to number nineteen in the US. 'Brothers In Arms' got to number sixteen in the UK. 'Walk Of Life' nearly didn't make it onto the *Brothers In Arms* album. Neil Dorfsman was against it being included but fortunately, he was outvoted by the rest of the band; a good thing considering that in the UK, it was Dire Straits' most commercially successful single from the album!

Melody Maker reviewed the single in January 1986; "It's hard to dislike Dire Straits, because you always end up admitting that Knopfler is a brilliant songwriter even if the songs aren't the kind that find their way into your own home. Besides, he's taken the piss out of Paula Yates on live television, which shows his vision and perspicacity in other ways too. 'Walk Of Life' boasts a good country swing, great hokey guitar and that intangible air of mellowness that to an untrained (or uninterested) ear makes all their songs sound the same. Attractive, if not one of their classics."

The tour that followed the release of *Brothers In Arms* was incredibly successful. Spanning across 1985 and 1986, over two and a half million tickets were sold. The tour covered Europe, Israel, North America, and Australia and New Zealand. Overall, Dire Straits played two hundred and forty-eight shows across over one hundred cities. Chris White joined the band on saxophone and the tour started on 25th April 1985 in Split,

Croatia (which was then part of Yugoslavia).

In response to being asked if it was necessary to train in preparation for a long tour, Knopfler told *Rolling Stone* in November 1985; "Oh, yes. I warm up on the rowing machine, and then I lift weights. You have to, or you'd be exhausted. I don't run — running's boring — but I've always loved sports. I played a little football when I was young, but I only started getting strong when I was seventeen or eighteen. The thing I like most about sports is hand-eye stuff, which I guess connects with playing guitar. I'm crazy about motor racing. I figure that if I didn't know how to play a note and didn't have any music in me, that's what I'd like to do. 'Cause that's an occupation guided by a very simple rule: Don't fuck up. It's always struck me as being very much to the point. It's obviously a rule that you apply to your rock and roll affairs as well. You've worked for your success in a very quiet, business-like manner. What happened with us is we became so successful quite quickly that we gathered up as much power as we could for ourselves. I would say that the vast majority of what you see is voluntary. I mean, you won't see us doing jingles for radio stations. I keep the making-music side of it as the main thing. Everything else is peripheral."

John Illsley said in *Musician* in September 1985; "The first leg of the tour is three months with hardly a day off. I'm just worried about somebody breaking a wrist or getting seriously ill. In seven years we've never cancelled a date. We just commit ourselves to a ludicrous schedule and try to stick to it."

Knopfler said; "We once had to put John onstage in a chair. In the very early days John decided he knew how to ride a horse. My brother David's girlfriend said, 'Let's go riding!' John said, 'I can do that!' Anyway, this horse took off down the field, jumped a haybale, and John went sailing off and landed on his back. Went straight to the hospital. We had a gig that night at the Albany Empire in Deptford. So we got him out of the hospital, gave him his bass, and stuck him onstage in a chair. He looked like King Arthur."

On 10th July 1985 when Dire Straits performed at Wembley Arena, they were accompanied by Nils Lofgren on 'Solid Rock' and by Hank Marvin on 'Going Home'. In January 1986, the performance was featured on Channel Four's *The Tube*. Whilst audio recordings of the performance have never been given an official release, bootleg recordings are in existence and go by the name of *Wembley Does The Walk Of Life*.

It was during their thirteen-night residency at Wembley Arena that on 13th July 1985, Dire Straits went down the road to Wembley Stadium to perform at *Live Aid*. Their iconic performance included 'Money For Nothing' with Sting joining them as guest vocalist. John Illsley recalled in 2019; "It was a very special feeling to be part of something so unique. *Live Aid* was a unique privilege for all of us. It's become a fabulous memory."

In 1985, a famine relief group led by John Abbey set out to walk from London to Khartoum to raise funds. The project was aptly named The Walk Of Life and Dire Straits donated a *Brothers In Arms* gold disc to the participants in recognition of their efforts. The last date of the *Brothers In Arms* tour was the 26th April 1986 at the Sydney Entertainment Centre. During the Australian leg of the tour, Dire Straits included impromptu renditions of 'Waltzing Matilda'. With 900,000 tickets sold across Australia and New Zealand, the scale of Dire Straits' tour of that part of the world was the biggest in music history. It wasn't until over 2017 and 2018 that Ed Sheeran broke this record.

From a journalist who got to witness one of the performances of the tour, it was reported in *New Musical Express* in January 1986; "Even the Second Coming would be hard-pressed to elicit a more committed public response from this audience. It's not too difficult to decipher The Straits' appeal: pub rock basics in a hi-tech setting. And, it's not just the terry-towel sweat bands that give Knopfler the mantle of athletic determination. For even the monotone dourness of his voice on such tracks as 'Private Investigations' and 'Walk Of Life' can't blunt his sharp-edged dexterity. He is to the guitar what Borg was to the tennis racket: the embodiment of the kind of rounded virtuosity that a silent majority aspire to. He's undoubtedly accounted for more guitar sales than his spiritual mentor Hank B. Marvin (with whom he shares his encore), courtesy of his often sublime, if sometimes skilfully-detached lines. Though capable of transcending the predictability of his entrenched traditionalism, Knopfler invariably applies the breaks (sic) when he should be high-flying."

On 8th April 1986, Dire Straits performed to a crowd of 17,000 in Darwin in Australia's Northern Territory. *The NT News* reported on the event. Notably, having spoken to a fan who was there, the article focussed on the weather to the point that it comes across that the gig was a bit of a washout but I am informed that from the fan's perspective, it was a great gig where the memory that has stayed with them is that of the music: "There wasn't a dry eye in the house, as they say, when supergroup Dire Straits faded from the stage after three hours of fine music last night. Unfortunately, not much else was dry either — although some disappointed Darwin drinkers might disagree. Steady rain set in soon after 7pm, leaving more than 17,000 Dire Straits fans in soaking disarray. Out came plastic garbage bags, blankets, bedspreads, tarpaulins, tonneau covers, soggy beer cartons, and all manner of items for shelter, but no one escaped a drenching as the evening wore on. The saturation situation was not improved by gatekeepers refusing to allow some people to take in umbrellas, on the rather spurious grounds they could be potentially dangerous. The heavens well and truly opened as thousands of concert goers poured towards the gates on their way home, negotiating fences, knee-deep puddles, overflowing gutters, boggy carparks and chaotic traffic. The rain put a damper on what was undoubtedly the most professionally staged concert Darwin has seen."

"It was also probably one of the soberest, thanks to a bar system which appeared designed to frustrate rather than refresh the many thirsty drinkers. They queued for hours to buy drink tickets, then queued again to collect drinks from the bar just metres away. Those buying for a group were angered they could collect only ten beer tickets at a time, then found they could be served only six beers at a time. Inadequate toilet facilities were another hazard with long queues of uncomfortable people waiting to use the grossly inadequate "conveniences"."

The Dire Straits boys didn't say much, just performed superbly and faultlessly. Unfortunately their soaring instrumentals and ballads could not be fully appreciated by some of the cold, wet crowd wallowing in a quagmire. Others let the rain trickle down their faces and clearly didn't care. Warming rock was what the people really wanted, the crowd enthusiastically welcoming danceable hits like 'Money For Nothing' and 'Tunnel Of Love'. The concert was nothing short of ecstasy for hundreds of fans packed into the area in front of the stage. The concert climaxed with a spectacular fireworks display which left the showgrounds swathed in smoke like a battlefield.

About forty police were on duty at the concert and on the roads later. They said the crowd was orderly, and no one — apart from one drunk taken into protective custody — was arrested. Several people were taken to hospital with minor injuries after six post-concert vehicle accidents. Dire Straits fans came from Mt Isa, Wyndham, Derby, Kununurra, Tennant Creek and Alice Springs for the concert. One bus load of patrons from Katherine had a long night of it when their bus broke down on the way back after the concert… Three bus loads came from Katherine. Those who missed the show had another chance to see the supergroup in action. Channel 8 showed a direct telecast of the final concert in Sydney later that month. Watching on the TV, it didn't have the atmosphere or the same superb sound but it was better than missing Dire Straits altogether.

Whilst the journalist's complaints about the setup of the venue are perhaps overzealous, it's important information in how it conveys the extent to which by 1986,

Performing on the French TV show Johnny Metro Blues in 1985.

John 6th July 1985 during one of the band's many performances at Wembley Arena.

Wembley Arena, 6th July 1985. This was the third of an astonishing twelve nights Dire Straits played at the Arena. The only night they didn't play between the 4th and the 16th was when they walked across the way to the Stadium for another little gig on the 13th, called Live Aid.

Dire Straits had hit the big time; they were playing excellently executed shows to crowds and venues so large that realistically, perhaps caused the music to be (quite literally) swamped by other factors outside of their control. Notably, the feature captioned photos of the concert: "Brilliant stage and lighting effects were a feature of the concert" and "lead singer Mark Knopfler showed why the group is the world's number one with his gravel-voiced vocals and driving guitar."

Interviewed backstage prior to a performance in Ottawa, Mark Knopfler said to *International Musician And Recording World* in January 1986; "I think this is the last of the big shows for us. We just did two weeks at Wembley Arena in London, and it's gotten to the point where you say, 'Well, I've done that.' Our promoter told me I could have done a month there, but you have to be crazy to do two weeks there anyway. So given the fact that we're already crazy, I don't see any reason to repeat it. Anything we do in the future is going to be much smaller; we'll do away with these massive PAs and lighting systems. I think that by the end of this tour I'll be more interested in playing small places and doing a different kind of thing altogether — if I go back to playing live."

It was reported in the same feature; "Dire Straits' present global assault is scheduled for over two hundred and twenty dates, and there's talk of even more being added. It's been estimated that the two-and-a-half-hour show costs in excess of $22,000 per day to put on and requires a crew of over sixty people. Things often don't go quite so smoothly. Backstage, small scenes begin to unfold, such as finding out that the two phones installed for band use both operate on the same line — a shouting match tells you one is not enough. A sigh is heard, a $50 piano-tuning bill is sighted, and on the bottom in red ink is a $15 additional charge for "waiting time"… The scope of Dire Straits' live show begins to take place at soundcheck… Knopfler strolls on stage and is handed his favourite red Schecter Stratocaster, Illsley straps on his '61 Fender Jazz bass, and Terry Williams parks himself behind a massive Ludwig/Simmons/Paiste drum kit. Fletcher and Clark are busy tuning oscillators. The PA is fired up, and the empty arena comes alive with various bits and pieces of the set. Second guitarist Jack Sonni, wiry, curly haired and sporting a loud Hawaiian shirt, bounds onto the stage and is handed his prize seafoam-green Schecter Stratocaster, and almost immediately the mood on stage changes. A recent addition to the band, in place of Hal Lindes, he radiates enough energy for both the entire group and crew. Knopfler cracks a rare smile and is handed his Gibson Les Paul Standard for a run-through of 'Money For Nothing'."

The Ottawa's Civic Centre gig was reviewed in the same feature; "The Dire Straits show starts out with a whimper instead of the usual bang, but you shiver nonetheless. The opening chords of 'Ride Across The River', a moody, slow-paced number, fairly hypnotise the crowd as Knopfler, dressed in his trademark red and black cowboy shirt and red headband, strolls out with a sunburst Strat and jumps into the opening lines. Illsley takes command of the left side of the stage and coaxes a beautiful low end out of his Fender Jazz bass, which he will play for the entire evening. Joined under the red glow of stage lights by a Stratocastered Jack Sonni, the group tears through 'Expresso Love', 'So Far Away' and 'Romeo And Juliet' without taking a breath. Knopfler's guitar playing has never sounded better."

Despite what Dire Straits achieved internationally with *Brothers In Arms* — in many parts of the world as well as the US — at the time, there was perhaps a sense that to have success in the US wasn't the holy grail. *Musician* wrote in September 1985; "Knopfler's a superstar in Europe, Asia and Australia. Dire Straits even enjoy great popularity in Latin America and the Middle East. If his band's substantial American success is not equal to the stature they enjoy elsewhere, it doesn't seem to bother Knopfler one bit. In fact, he takes a sort of perverse pleasure from his low American profile. When Dire Straits made their last studio album, 1982's *Love Over Gold*, the band asked Warner Bros. to release as a single 'Telegraph Road', a track that lasted fourteen minutes. Dire Straits last toured the US in 1980. Five years later, they've finally consented to make another pass."

Knopfler said; "The fact that we don't *have* to "break America" has become one of the main reasons we don't. It would be great if we had a bigger audience here in the States, but it's very nice as it is. We do have a big audience here. It's not anything like other countries, but we're not going to kill ourselves in Holiday Inns in order to achieve it 'cause once you do, so what? We don't feel we have to play the Astrodome. We do enough of these gigs in the rest of the world. We enjoy them, they're events. But a lot of these acts who are trying to make it in the States just seem like rats in a barrel, scrambling for every bit of billboard space, air space, chart space. I mean, I think I'd be a liar if I said it didn't bother me that so much mundane stuff is being touted as the greatest thing — but hey, you know, it's popular. I was just told that we're apparently one of Warners' top selling acts over here."

It is understandable Mark Knopfler may have been more well known in the US than the other Dire Straits. Of course, he was the frontman of the band but there were also other factors at play. It was asserted in *Musician* in September 1985; "To the American public Mark Knopfler *is* Dire Straits. He writes and sings all the group's songs, produces their albums, and plays the distinctive, haunting guitar that is the band's sonic signature. In the five years since Dire Straits last played in this country Knopfler's name has been before the public as a record producer (Bob Dylan's *Infidels*, Aztec Camera's *Knife*), a film composer (*Local Hero, Cal, Comfort And Joy*) and session guitarist (Van Morrison's *Beautiful Vision*, Steely Dan's *Gaucho*, Bryan Ferry's *Boys And Girls* and a host of others). The other Dire Straits only recent American splash was as Tina Turner's backing band on 'Private Dancer', a song written by *Mark Knopfler*."

John Illsley was quoted in the same feature; "Mark does between sixty and seventy five percent of the music in the band. The rest is worked out by the guys. I do an awful lot of the administration and stuff. I'm the link between the band and the management. I also just filter out a lot of stuff, make non-musical decisions. Mark trusts me to do that. I think we're a good team. I think we complement each other musically, too. I'm an emotional bass player. I respond to the song and ideas. The parts are worked out real carefully. So when somebody starts to mess around with them it throws everybody off. The last keyboard player we added would learn his part, play it in rehearsal, and then when we got on stage we'd all go 'What was *that?*' If we were a blues band, okay — but when we play something like 'Romeo And Juliet' you can't mess about."

In contrast to the scale of Dire Straits' success, Mark Knopfler's passion for the music itself was a key motivation. *Rolling Stone* reported in November 1985; "The group has long been a superstar attraction in England, Europe, Australia and Japan. Now, the smash hit 'Money For Nothing' has given the band its first number one album in America; *Brothers In Arms* has already sold two million copies. But Mark Knopfler has rarely been seen in public without a guitar around his neck since he founded Dire Straits in the summer of 1977 as a vehicle for his evocative country-and-blues-rooted songs. Offstage, his life seems to be an endless succession of Dire Straits recording sessions, film soundtracks and guest appearances on other artists' records."

Knopfler said; "Even now I just go up and look at my guitars sitting on the side of the stage. I'll hang out at Rudy's Music Stop down on Forty-Eighth Street when I'm in town, just to be around the instruments, just looking at the damn things."

When asked if stardom was something that he had explicitly pursued, Knopfler was quoted in *Rolling Stone* in November 1985; "Oh, no. That's a by-product of a love affair with a guitar and wanting to be in a band and make music. I always wanted to be in a band. I used to draw pictures of bands when I was a little kid in school. I used to draw pictures of guitars all day. I used to go and watch a guy in the woodwork room making a guitar, just so I could hold it. I pestered my dad for years and years until I got a cheap imitation one. It was a red imitation Stratocaster. He bought it for me on my fifteenth birthday. It cost fifty pounds, which was a lot then."

At the age of thirteen, Knopfler had played the violin. "I could get great-sounding notes out of it, but don't ask me to read music. I tried the saxophone a couple of years ago, but it's so much tied in with reading that it's impossible for me. I go by my ears. I can't relate music to those dots. I found out more about music in the past few years just by studying chords. You learn them the same way you do words. You hear a long word and you know what it means just by its usage. Your vocabulary increases. The same way with chords. I can recognise music now that I couldn't have four years ago."

On where he saw himself being in twenty years' time, Knopfler said; "I'll be in clubs, playing. I'll fall over onstage, dead, someday. I'd like to work on a smaller scale again, play some small clubs. I got together with J.J. Cale in a club in San Francisco not long ago and had a really good time. I got up with the Everly Brothers in a club in Canada. They recorded 'Why Worry', from *Brothers In Arms*, and I played a few songs with them… If I ever get the chance to sit around at home, I return to certain artists again and again. Like Van Morrison. I think even something recent of his, like *Inarticulate Speech Of The Heart*, is fabulous. 'Rave On, John Donne' is a magnificent song. I like J.J. Cale a lot. I like the rough textures of his records."

The passion for music in and of itself was plausibly a key motivation point for all of the band. John Illsley told *Musician* in September 1985; "I'm almost totally impressed by amazing players. Sometimes the whole technique thing just knocks the soul out of music. You're not thinking about feeling, gut reaction. You're thinking about technique. So you produce something that goes over most people's heads. Oh yeah, it's great playing. But touch something here." (he pointed to his chest re *here*).

Knopfler said in the same feature; "I don't believe in perfect. There's so many ways to do any song. Perfection's just a cloud in the air. People say I'm a perfectionist. It's just not so… I have the self-confidence to go gaily steaming off in completely the wrong direction. Yes, that's the kind of man I am. Musically, it's very easy for things to get out of hand with me. Just because I've got the confidence. I continually put myself in situations where it's made absolutely obvious that the directions I feel like charging off in aren't the right directions at all. Neil's probably lost count of the times that I've been working away quite happily with something and he's had to say, 'It's not really working.' It's always most humbling, educational and delightful to learn that you are in fact wrong."

The scale of the *Brothers In Arms* tour was such that once it ended, Mark Knopfler elected to focus on solo projects, film soundtracks and producing. In 1987, he did the production on Willy DeVille's album, *Miracle*. On balance though, the *Brothers In Arms* tour was possibly right for what Mark Knopfler wanted to do at the time: "I'd like to move now away from these little excursions into writing film scores and producing other people, and just tour with the band and then make another Dire Straits album. To me the band is the best thing. I've always enjoyed it more than anything else. And of course, you know I'm very slow. I have to do all these other things to find out just how much the band means to me. I'm so slow that I have to be bashed over the head more than once; I have to learn the nuts and bolts of record production to figure out that I don't really get off on record production. It's when I'm rehearsing with the band that I'm totally in tune with what's going on. That's when I really am happiest. Making a record is beautiful when it's happening. But when it's not happening — for any reason — it can be a diabolical pain."

And of course, when with the band, there was a sense of camaraderie:-"Everybody says bands are a pain. But it's worth it. I realised that the first time I went out and did a session with somebody else. It's always great to get back to the band. If I went in to do a solo record and I wasn't feeling good that day and all I had was a bunch of hired people, it would be hard. Peer pressure can keep the ball rolling, keep the vibe going. And you'd be alone a lot of the time. If you had to do a TV show you'd turn up by yourself, you'd be travelling through Germany in winter with a bunch of hired hands. You'd sit in airport lounges by yourself. With Dire Straits we all see things at the same time. I travel through an ever-changing world with *shared* eyes."

And in *International Musician And Recording World* in January 1986 Knopfler said; "The road is great, though you really have to love it, you really have to be into it. Sure, some of the lows are pretty low, but they're not worth talking about because this band is so fabulous. We had trouble with the keyboards for a while, but Guy Fletcher and the crew are so together that things are fine now."

If Dire Straits weren't a household name before, *Brothers In Arms* had soon put paid to that. As amazing as the achievement was, along with all of the doors that it opened up for the band, the demand of the workload relating to it was stratospheric — so much so, that an element of exhaustion certainly became part and parcel of the whole thing. Mark Knopfler told *Record Collector* in May 2019; "I think things reach a critical mass. I'd always enjoyed touring — the travel, the crew, the banter, the whole thing. And I was always very confident about being in charge of it: that came naturally. But when it got that big, suddenly there were three different stages, twenty extra crew whose names I didn't know, more this, more that — it just didn't feel right to me. The scale of it. It wasn't the same thing. Plus, I was very tired. I was burned out. I felt like a frayed sweater. Holes everywhere. You need to go home and knit yourself together again, if you can."

It is understandable as to why the band felt like they needed a rest. Upon being asked, "As rock stars go, you seem to be all work and no play. Would you say you're a workaholic, that you do music to the exclusion of all else?" Knopfler said in *Rolling Stone* in November 1985; "I wish that wasn't the case. Because I like all the things that guys like. You know, I love to eat and I love to sleep. I love to watch sports, I like cars. But when you're touring so much and doing all these things, it ends up that you haven't got time to put in new light bulbs all over the place. I just don't get off on painting the toilet. I get accused of being lazy. I'm lying on the bed, watching sports on TV, and Lourdes (his wife at the time) wants me off the bed, she wants to tidy up around me. I end up getting thrown out of the house. You have to go do something, right? So why not go do a session?"

Dire Straits regrouped to perform at Wembley Stadium on 11th June 1988 at Nelson Mandela's seventieth birthday tribute concert. As the headline act, they were joined on their set by Eric Clapton who performed his hit song, 'Wonderful Tonight'. It wasn't long after that Williams left Dire Straits. In the September of that year, Mark Knopfler announced the official split of Dire Straits. He was quoted in *Rolling Stone*; "A lot of press reports were saying we were the biggest band in the world. There's not an accent then on the music, there's an accent on popularity. I needed a rest."

In the October, a Dire Straits greatest hits compilation was released. Titled *Money For Nothing*, it got to number one in the UK. The band's first hit single, 'Sultans Of Swing', was re-released as a single in the UK to promote the album. The same year saw John Illsley release his second album, *Glass*. It featured Mark Knopfler, Alan Clark, Guy Fletcher and Chris White as guest musicians.

On 9th October 1989 Dire Straits made a surprise appearance at Newcastle's Mayfair Ballroom for a charity concert in honour of Joanne Gillespie. The eleven year old was the National Children of Courage and North East Personality award winner having published her book, *Brave Heart,* about her fight against cancer. The concert raised more than £35,000.

It was towards the end of the decade that Mark Knopfler formed The Notting

Hillbillies. The band's line-up — across varying combinations thereof — featured Guy Fletcher, Brendan Croker, Paul Franklin, Marcus Cliffe and Steve Phillips as well as manager Ed Bicknell on drums. With a country music feel, released in 1990, the band's only album, *Missing...Presumed Having A Good Time* spawned the minor hit single 'Your Own Sweet Way'. For the rest of 1990, The Notting Hillbillies toured and made an appearance on *Saturday Night Live*. Knopfler's focus on country music was further apparent in his collaboration with Chet Atkins for their 1990 album, *Neck And Neck*.

In 1990, Dire Straits performed at Knebworth Festival. Alongside Eric Clapton and Elton John, they played 'Solid Rock', 'Money For Nothing', and 'I Think I Love You Too Much'. Knopfler stated that as an experimental song, he wasn't confident in the possibility of releasing the latter on record. He thus gifted it to Canadian blues/jazz artist Jeff Healey at a time when it wasn't known that a Dire Straits reunion would be on the cards. Healey recorded it for his 1990 album, *Hell To Pay*.

John Illsley who, like Mark Knopfler was a constant throughout the entire Dire Straits career.

John Illsley flanked by Ray Cooper and Elton John being introduced to Prince Charles at the Prince's Trust Rock Party: 10th anniversary at Wembley Arena, 20th June 1986. Although Dire Straits didn't perform John and Mark were part of a startling ensemble under the name of The Prince's All Stars. The rest of the line-up was Phil Collins (drums), Ray Cooper (percussion), Mark King of Level 42 (bass), Elton John (piano), Howard Jones (keyboards), Eric Clapton, Midge Ure and Bryan Adams (guitars).

*Mark with special guest Eric Clapton at the
Nelson Mandela 70th Birthday Tribute concert at
Wembley Stadium, 11th June 1988*

Wembley Stadium, 11th June 1988

Backstage at the Mayfair Ballroom, Newcastle. The band performed a special show in front of just 700 people. The concert was in support of North East Personality of the Year, twelve-year old Joanne Gillespie who wrote the book Brave Heart about her fight against cancer.
Joanne with her tongue out and friends from left Alan Clark, Terry Williams, John Illsley, Sarah Gillespie, Mark Knopfler, Chris White, Guy Fletcher, and Brendan Croker, 9th October 1989. It was Dire Straits only performance that year.

Mark examining his guitar during the last tour at Gateshead International Stadium, 13th June 1992.

6

On Every Street

Dire Straits got back together in early 1991. With Ed Bicknell still in the role as manager, the band line-up consisted of just four people once again: Alan Clark, Guy Fletcher, John Illsley and Mark Knopfler. They set to work on making a new album with Knopfler and Clark as producers. Dire Straits welcomed a number of session musicians to the recording. Paul Franklin contributed steel guitar and Danny Cummings did percussion. Chris White returned on saxophone and Phil Palmer played guitar. In place of Terry Williams on drums was Jeff Porcaro of Toto fame. For the world tour that followed the album, Chris Whitten played drums.

On Every Street — Dire Straits' sixth (and final) studio album — was released in the September of 1991. It was met with a mixed reception but nevertheless, it got to number one in not only the UK but in several European countries (it was certified diamond in France) as well as Australia. It got to number twelve in the US. By 2008, it had sold fifteen million copies. The album did astonishingly well despite a number of derogatory reviews.

Pennsylvania's *Daily News* considered in January 1992, "Depending on how well you like a musical smorgasbord, the Dire Straits' first album since 1985 is remarkable either for its diversity or lack of focus. No one is going to accuse leader Mark Knopfler of being stuck in a rut, that's for certain. *On Every Street* includes rockabilly ('The Bug'), MTV rock ('Heavy Fuel'), cocktail-lounge jazz ('Fade To Black'), folk music ('Iron Hand'), country ('How Long'), lush strings ('Ticket To Heaven') and swinging horns ('My Parties'). The band spares us any rap. Pulling this potential mess together are Knopfler's laid-back singing, jaw-dropping guitar licks and wry humour. 'My Parties' and 'Heavy Fuel' are Straitfaced satire more worthy of a bookshelf than a record rack."

A number of the singles from *On Every Street* had success in Europe, the US and Australia but despite this, none of them did well in the UK. The first single from the album was an edited version of 'Calling Elvis'. The single was supported with a video directed by Gerry Anderson, based on his TV show, *Thunderbirds*. Although the single did get to number twenty-one in the UK upon the first week of its release, within four weeks, it had dropped out of the charts there completely.

In other parts of the world though, 'Calling Elvis' hit the top ten throughout Europe as well as in Australia and New Zealand. Notably, it got to number one in Italy and to number two in Sweden and Denmark. *Music & Media* reviewed 'Calling Elvis' in August 1991; "Returning to recording after a six-year hiatus, Knopfler and Co. are about to challenge the success of *Brothers In Arms*. This is the first single of the *On Every Street* release. The song has the same shuffle rhythm as 'Southbound Again', a track on their 1978 debut album."

The following single, 'Heavy Fuel', didn't touch the top fifty in the UK but in the US it got to number one on Billboard's Mainstream Rock Tracks chart (it was Dire Straits' second song to reach this achievement, with the first having been 'Money For Nothing'). 'Heavy Fuel' also hit the top twenty in Canada and Belgium and the top thirty in Australia. *Music & Media* reviewed 'Heavy Fuel' in November 1991; "The second single off *On Every Street* is the same kind of rocker as 1985's 'Money For Nothing'. New on this song about fast food is the combination of ZZ Top-styled rocking guitars with the sound of steel guitar."

The title track from *On Every Street* also struggled to make an impact in the UK. It failed to reach the top forty. It got to number twenty-five in France though. The final single released from *On Every Street* in the UK was 'The Bug'. Backing vocals for the song were contributed by Vince Gill. Dire Straits invited him to join them as a full member but he declined in favour of wanting to focus on his solo career.

On Every Street was reviewed in *The New York Times* in September 1991; "From their self-titled 1978 debut through their new album, *On Every Street*, Dire Straits have been responsible for some of the prettiest moments in all of rockdom. 'Romeo And Juliet', from their 1980 album *Making Movies*, tried to answer age-old questions about love with a starry-toned mandolin melody and lines like 'All I do is kiss you through the bars of a rhyme.' The 1982 opus *Love Over Gold* reconciled violently opposed musical extremes, from a drum beat resounding like thunder to a piano trickling like water in a gutter. Even the simplest clichés, like the it'll-be-all-right sentiment of 'Why Worry', from the 1985 megahit *Brothers In Arms*, were vested with enough emotion to elevate them above the ordinary."

"Mark Knopfler, the band's lead singer, songwriter, producer and guitar wizard, seemed bent on transforming rock into an idiom capable of near-operatic beauty; Dire Straits albums sounded as though Mr Knopfler had examined life's great truths under a microscope and wanted to project what he found onto the very heavens above. In the six years since the release of *Brothers In Arms*, Dire Straits have toured one hundred and seventeen cities and played to world audiences at events like *Live Aid*. Mr Knopfler indulged his penchant for sonic vistas by composing the film scores of *The Colour of Money*, *The Princess Bride* and *Last Exit To Brooklyn*. Then he recorded two side projects: *Neck And Neck*, an album of duets with the country-western guitarist Chet Atkins, and an off-the-cuff collection of traditional songs with the Notting Hillbillies, a kind of poor-man's Travelling Wilburys."

"Mr Knopfler's lengthy hiatus has not led him to rethink Dire Straits' direction; if anything, it has allowed him to peg the band's sound more certainly. 'Calling Elvis', the opening track of *On Every Street*, rises so cleanly from the fade-out of the last track of *Brothers In Arms*, the two songs could almost be adjacent on the same album. The new recording includes the same super-sophisticated guitar arpeggios, epic synthesiser backdrops, brooding ballads and intricate production techniques that have defined Dire Straits since 1980. The album has neither the bouncy, unapologetic pop of songs like 'Walk Of Life', nor the immense sweep of 'Telegraph Road', from *Love Over Gold*, but rather a deft, middle-of-the-road compromise between the two."

"In his lyrics, Mr Knopfler continues to gripe about lust, greed, corruption, capitalism, dirty money, empty hearts, broken hearts, blood-stained battlefields, starving children, television evangelists. On the lyric sheet, each song title is designed to look like a postmark, as if the songs were letters from different states of the mind. But the lyrics also re-tread a surprising amount from past albums. *On Every Street* lacks the complex metaphorical layers of its predecessors; Mr Knopfler has always valued universal over personal experience, but here his imagery seems washed out. 'Fade To Black' reworks an idea from *Making Movies* to lesser effect, while 'Heavy Fuel' and 'My Parties' reprise the cynicism and social satire of the band's biggest hit, 'Money For Nothing'. The title track updates the *Love Over Gold* song 'Private Investigations', and there's even a 'Brothers In Arms'-style war song, 'Iron Hand'. *On Every Street* is Dire Straits' least ambitious album. Mr Knopfler's past achievements lay in his ability to stretch the rock idiom, expand it — to use rock's limitations as his starting point. Here he seems content to work within boundaries. The fact that the album's prettiest song, the string-drenched ballad 'Ticket To Heaven', is actually a send-up of televangelism feels like something of a cheat. *On Every Street* offers no great truths, only observances."

It was reviewed in *Music & Media* in the same month; "Happily, Knopfler and Co.'s first album in six years isn't *Brothers In Arms* part two, but it gives a good taste of all the different projects Knopfler has been working on since. His collaboration with Chet Atkins shines through clearly, with steel guitars enriching the overall sound, leading it as never before towards country. The band play a wide variety of styles, ranging from lazy slow blues in 'Fade To Black' and 'You And Your Friend' to J.J. Cale-styled and economically-played rock in 'When It Comes To You', while 'Heavy Fuel' listens like ZZ Top in Nashville. 'The Iron Hand' is the type of anti-Thatcher political song you would expect from any lonesome hobo, 'Ticket To Heaven', with loads of violins, should be an instant hit for the days around Christmas."

On 23rd August 1991, starting in Dublin, Dire Straits embarked on a world tour that continued up until a performance in Spain on 9th October 1992. The scale of the tour was such that the band played to some 7.1 million ticket holders across three hundred shows.

In February 1992, *The New York Times* reviewed a performance that took place at Brendan Byrne Arena in East Rutherford, New Jersey; "If Dire Straits hadn't been right there onstage on Sunday night, you might have thought you were sitting at home listening to the group's albums on the stereo. The sound was digitally perfect, mixed so that the singer Mark Knopfler's guitar notes were always at the forefront. The songs, spanning the band's recording history from 'Sultans Of Swing' in 1978 to the latest album, *On Every Street*, were often flawless reproductions of the studio originals. The audience was polite and restrained; no one stood up, no one yelled or whistled in the quiet parts. The only things missing were a couch, to stretch out on and maybe doze a little, and a remote control, to skip over the boring songs, of which there were many."

"Despite the enormous popularity attained with the 1985 blockbuster *Brothers In Arms*, Dire Straits essentially makes private music. As a songwriter, Mr Knopfler frequently works at a decibel level barely above a whisper, and his slow, hushed numbers are constructed from instrumental minutiae like delicate guitar fills, tinkling piano and long patches with nothing but the breath of a synthesiser. Even his hits have a painstaking precision; he seems to use fat power chords only when he wants to make a joke about rock-and-roll, as in the heavily ironic 'Money For Nothing'. Attempting to translate this into a live situation, Dire Straits became bogged down in a morass of textures and snail's-pace tempos. The nine-piece band, spread across a two-tiered stage, consisted of two drummers, three guitarists, a bassist, two keyboardists and a horn player. The two-and-

Mark made a return visit to his old stamping ground at Archibald First School in Gosforth, Newcastle and met staff, parents and children. He was back in his native North East to receive a honorary doctorate from Newcastle University, 7th May 1993.

Mark in London on 30th March 2000 with the OBE he received at Buckingham Palace from the Prince of Wales.

Return of the Café Racers? Trying out a new bike in 2001.

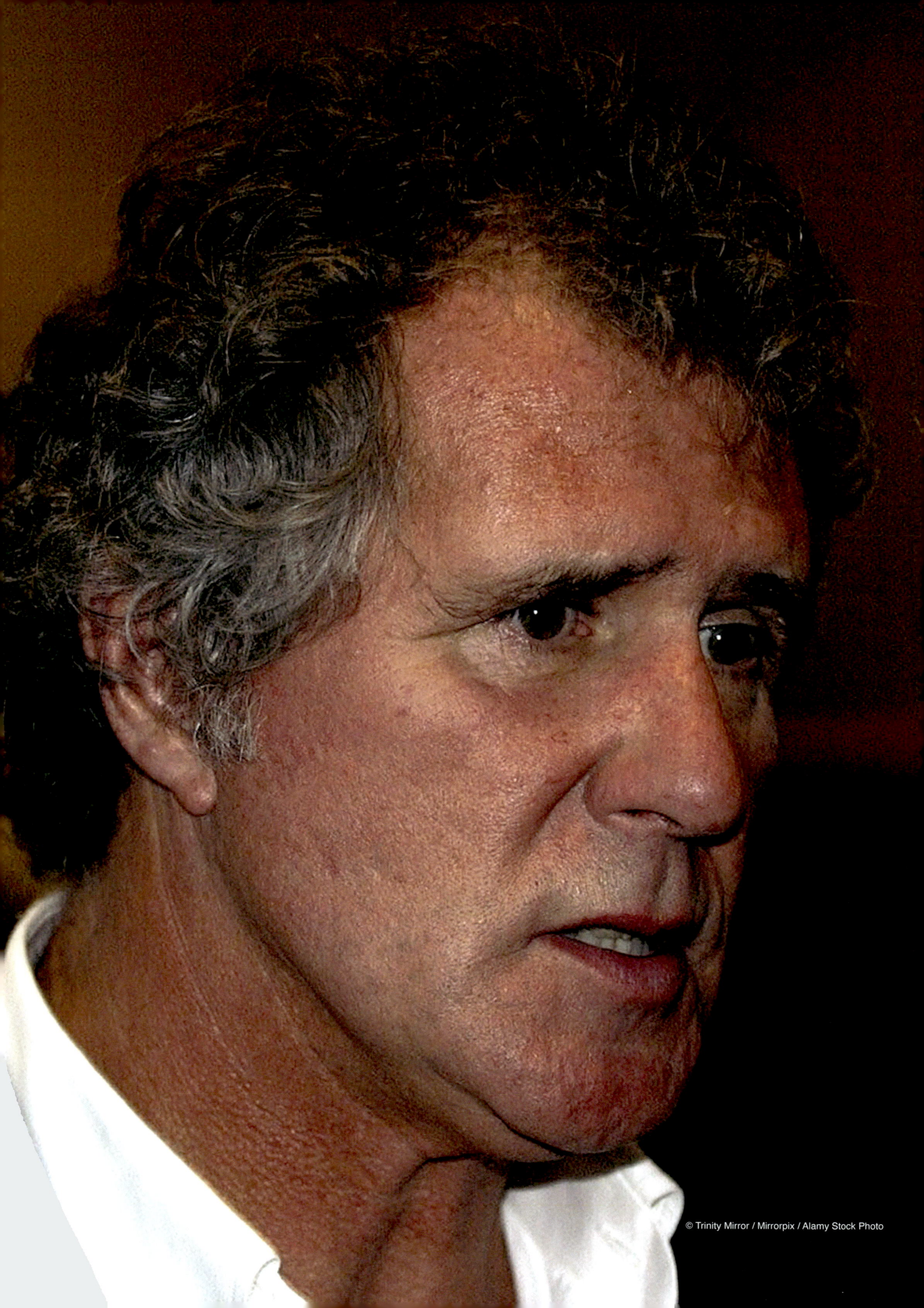

John Illsley at Mark Knopfler's Tribute day at Newcastle Civic Centre, 19th October 2006. The Variety Club presented Mark with their highest accolade, the Silver Heart, at a special Tribute Lunch held at the Civic Centre in Newcastle-upon-Tyne.

Around 700 people packed the Banqueting Hall to hear Jools Holland MC the Tribute with contributions from John amongst others, including fellow Geordies Jimmy Nail, Tim Healey, Alan Shearer, and Shadows guitarist, Bruce Welch. Mark spoke about his early life, of growing up in Newcastle and his deep affection for Northumberland. Mark and Guy Fletcher also performed 'Wild Theme' from the Local Hero album at the end of the afternoon.

Mark Knopfler and John Illsley on 3rd December 2009 unveil a plaque outside 1 Farrer House in Deptford, South London, the venue for Dire Straits first gig.

John Illsley, Alan Clark, and Guy Fletcher on the red carpet before the 2018 Rock and Roll Hall of Fame Induction Ceremony, Saturday, April 14th, 2018, in Cleveland. Mark Knopfler declined the invitation to attend.

a-half-hour show opened with what would customarily be a finale: a lengthy extended jam on 'Calling Elvis', from *On Every Street*, which went on for so long it almost needed an intermission afterward. Everyone took solos, including both drummers. Multicoloured lights danced off every fret and cymbal, giving the stage the look of a kind of exotic aquarium."

"Elsewhere, Mr Knopfler put in jams where there were no songs. 'Sultans Of Swing', for which shadowy crew members brought out a third, smaller drum kit so that Mr Knopfler could affect the intimacy of a garage band, ended and then started again as a different tune before Mr Knopfler had worked back to the original melody. New ballads like 'Fade To Black' and 'Planet Of New Orleans' were so sluggish and monstrously uncompelling that their inclusion seemed pointless. Only in a few places did Mr Knopfler inject some real human warmth into the show. He played a gorgeous steel-guitar lead in 'Romeo And Juliet', from 1980's *Making Movies*; pedal steel guitar added a country tinge to the ditty 'Walk Of Life'. 'Two Young Lovers', from the 1983 'Twisting By The Pool', was a noble choice, but it showed how far Dire Straits has come from spontaneous, rough-and-tumble rock-and-roll. For most bands, live shows are an opportunity to bring out the heart and soul that might be missing from their recordings; for Dire Straits it worked in reverse."

The Vancouver Sun reported in April 1992; "Mark Knopfler is a man who knows what he wants and how to get it. In return, he gave it back to 12,500 fans Tuesday during the first of two sold out nights at the Coliseum. As writer/producer/singer and guitarist-extraordinaire for chart-topping British rockers Dire Straits, Knopfler has led his band through a fourteen-year career distinguished by a variety of personnel changes, a whack of massive-selling albums and a string of hit singles. In the same capacity, he led an eight-piece outfit through an aurally intense pristine two hour performance showcasing his various — and formidable — talents. Arriving on stage amid a swirl of multicoloured lasers that seemed out of place against his everyman's attire of trademark headband, blue jeans and button-down shirt, Knopfler and company launched directly into 'Calling Elvis', a hit from their first album in six years, 1991's *On Every Street*."

"Dire Straits is a band that likes to jam. 'Calling Elvis' lasted almost fifteen minutes before it hit 'Walk Of Life', the smash hit from 1985's multiplatinum selling *Brothers In Arms*. Explaining that they were 'just getting warmed up,' the band members — Knopfler, bassist John Illsley, keyboardist Alan Clark and drummer Guy Fletcher, along with an additional keyboardist, a second guitarist, a pedal-steel player, a sax player and a percussionist — went on to demonstrate their respective chops throughout the night. While it was mighty fine of them to do so, as all are accomplished musicians, there's no getting around the fact that, unless you're completely stoked on Knopfler's vision and dexterity on the fretboard, it can become tiresome. Knopfler, of course, has written great songs: 'Romeo And Juliet', 'Telegraph Road', 'On Every Street' — all performed Tuesday evening — evoke visions of colourful yet tragic figures on par with those created by Dylan and Springsteen. As a guitarist, he possesses an oft-imitated yet ultimately inimitable style, readily adapted to the flavour of his tunes, ranging from rock to pop to country to jazz to flamenco to whatever. But Dire Straits' tendency toward epic-like marathons makes the band somewhat difficult to sit through for the casual fan in an arena atmosphere. There were, however, some unexpected highlights: country singer John Anderson joined the band for an inspired version of 'When It Comes To You', and only the original 1978-sized quartet of guitar, guitar, bass and drums remained on stage for a snazzier, less jazzy take on 'Sultans Of Swing'. By that point, the otherwise sedate, late twenties-ish, early thirties-ish crowd had got to its feet and was howling along with Knopfler's gruff talk-sing right through to the encore of 'Money For Nothing'."

"The tour was more musically enhanced than Dire Straits' previous world tour but despite this, it wasn't as commercially successful. Still though, the *On Every Street* tour was equally demanding for the band and as a result, Mark Knopfler had had enough of being committed to something of such scale. Consequently, this was a catalyst for Dire Straits' second and final split."

Regarding *On Every Street*, Alan Clark recalled in 2014; "I was surprised that we did that record, actually — because after *Brothers In Arms*, I thought that might very well be the end of Dire Straits. Because I think for Mark, it would have been a great idea to leave it on a massive high like *Brothers In Arms* was. Mark was very interested in doing his solo projects. He was also very interested in producing other people and doing movie scores. I think if things had worked out differently, then that might have been it, actually. The songs that made it onto the *On Every Street* record may well have become a solo record for Mark. It's hard for me to say, but I think that really one of the reasons why Mark decided to keep the band together and make that record was because he was going through a divorce — and I think it kind of got him out of the house. I think it gave him a good distraction and kept him busy and out on the road."

With the advantage of hindsight, Ed Bicknell asserted in later years that the tour hadn't been an enjoyable experience due to the initial excitement to do it no longer there. Not only that, but the band members were struggling with personal relationships outside of the band. The emotional and physical strain of doing a world tour lasting nearly two years plus not having the time and space to have a proper break took its toll on everyone concerned.

Alan Clark said; "Back in 1992 I had pretty much had enough of playing Dire Straits songs because Dire Straits used to go out on the road for a long time. So in 1992, I was quite happy to take a break."

By the end of the *On Every Street* tour, Mark Knopfler was candid about the fact that he no longer wished to embark on large scale touring anymore. His exhaustion was such that he took a break from the music business. He was quoted in *The Telegraph* in September 2012; "I put the thing to bed because I wanted to get back to some kind of reality. It's self-protection, a survival thing. That kind of scale is dehumanising."

In May 1993, the live album, *On The Night*, was released. It features performances from the *On Every Street* tour. Despite being met with mixed reviews, the album reached the top five in the UK — a noteworthy achievement for any live album. Also in May 1993, the *Encores* EP was released. Consisting of four tracks, it got to number one in France and Spain and to number thirty-one in the UK. Dire Straits' final album, *Live At The BBC*, features a range of live recordings spanning from 1978 to 1981, most of which feature the original line-up of the band. The album was released in June 1995 as part of Dire Straits still having contractual obligations of Vertigo Records. It was around this time that Mark Knopfler set to work on what would be his full solo album.

Mark Knopfler released his debut as a solo artist, *Golden Heart*, in March 1996. It was his first solo album having worked on collaborative projects for nearly two decades. The success of Dire Straits still followed him into his solo career, for it was in the August of 1996 that *Brothers In Arms* was certified nine times platinum in the US. It was also during 1996 that Bob Ludwig remastered the whole Dire Straits catalogue for release on CD.

On 19th June 1999 Mark Knopfler, John Illsley, Alan Clark and Guy Fletcher got together for a final time. With Ed Bicknell on drums, they played five songs for Illsley's wedding. The set included a rendition of Chuck Berry's 'Nadine'.

In 2002, Mark Knopfler, John Illsley, Guy Fletcher, Danny Cummings and Chris White got together for four charity concerts. During the first half, Knopfler was joined by Brendan Croker; they mostly played The Notting Hillbillies' songs. At the performance in Shepherd's Bush, Jimmy Nail contributed backing vocals to Knopfler's solo piece, 'Why Aye Man'. 'Why Aye Man' features on Knopfler's album released in that year, *The*

Ragpicker's Dream. The album strongly references various aspects of Knopfler's home place, the North East of England.

In November 2005, Dire Straits' most recent compilation album was released, *Private Investigations: The Best Of Dire Straits & Mark Knopfler*. It got into the UK top twenty. As well as featuring songs from Dire Straits' discography, it also includes some of Mark Knopfler's solo and soundtrack work. Two editions of the album were released; a single CD with a grey cover and double CD with a blue cover. A previously unreleased track, a duet with Emmylou Harris, 'All The Roadrunning', was included on the album. When *Brothers In Arms* was rereleased in 2005 as a limited edition twentieth anniversary edition, the success of it was such that it won a Grammy for Best Surround Sound Album.

In 2006, Mark Knopfler opened a recording studio in Chiswick. Called British Grove, it has played host to a number of high-profile artists including The Rolling Stones, David Gilmour, Duffy and Travis. It was also used by Disney to work on a score for a new project relating to *Aladdin*. Knopfler was quoted in *Record Collector* in May 2019; "The philosophy there is the best of the old and the best of the new. If you want to make records in the great tradition, the standards are kept up. Giving something back is great."

Over the years since the Dire Straits' breakup, Mark Knopfler has been candid about his reservations on getting the band back together. He was quoted in a BBC News article in October 2008; "It just got too big. If anyone can tell me one good thing about fame, I'd be very interested to hear it."

Regarding Knopfler's stance, John Illsley was quoted in the same feature; "He says 'Oh, I don't know whether to start getting all that stuff back together again'… Mark and I were the only two left in '93, so it's really up to him and I if it happens at all, but he's doing incredibly well as a solo artist, so hats off to him. He's having a perfectly good time doing what he's doing."

On his website, Guy Fletcher also stipulated that Mark Knopfler has no desire to reform Dire Straits. Released in October 2008, John Illsley released an album with Irish musician Greg Pearle — *Beautiful You*. The album was the product of a two-year collaboration.

Although not working under the Dire Straits name, Guy Fletcher has worked on the majority of Mark Knopfler's solo material to date. Also, Danny Cummings has been a regular contributor. In particular, he has played on Knopfler's recent solo albums: *All The Roadrunning* (with Emmylou Harris), *Kill To Get Crimson*, *Get Lucky* and *Down The Road Wherever*.

In December 2009, Dire Straits were commemorated with a Heritage award from PRS (Performing Right Society) for Music. The plaque was put on a block of flats (outside the ground floor of Farrer House, Church Street) in London's Deptford — the very place where Dire Straits played their first gig (albeit as the Café Racers). Mark Knopfler and John Illsley attended the unveiling ceremony.

In 2011, for the purpose of performing at a charity show at the Royal Albert Hall, Alan Clark, Chris White, and Phil Palmer, along with Tom Petty and the Heartbreakers' drummer Steve Ferrone, formed a new band named The Straits.

In December 2017, it was announced that Dire Straits would be inducted into the Rock And Roll Hall Of Fame in 2018. Illsley was quoted in *Billboard* in December 2017; "It fills me with a lot of pleasure to be recognised and to be included in the thing that we love doing best, which is making music and playing rock n' roll." Regarding the scope of a reunion performance, he was quoted in the same feature; "Mark is quite sort of restrained about things like this. We have spoken about (the induction), and we just said, 'Oh, that's nice.' I think it would probably be important if Mark and I were there. I'll definitely be there, and I'll definitely talk Mark into coming as well. It's essentially up to him if he wants to do anything, and I completely respect his feelings about it. He doesn't want too much white light."

Mark Knopfler didn't attend the ceremony. When asked to discuss the reasons behind it, endearingly, Illsley was quoted in *Music Radar* in September 2020; "I'll assure you it's a personal thing. Let's just leave it at that." Of Dire Straits, only Clark, Fletcher and Illsley attended the ceremony.

Perhaps some of the formalities of musicianship were never likely to appeal to Mark Knopfler who was seemingly, in it for the music itself. He was quoted in *Rolling Stone* in November 1985; "The thing about my guitar playing is that I don't know much about it. It's a process of always learning stuff. I recently went down to Nashville to play with Chet Atkins on an album he's making of duets with other guitarists. I could have stayed there for five years. I loved it and learned so much. So it never ends, what you need to learn. In terms of my vocabulary with the guitar, I think I can say, 'Hello, how are you?' and that's about it. I basically feel that as long as you have soul and you have melody, then it doesn't matter whether you're Miles Davis or Waylon Jennings. You're going to make good music. Often, you find that very advanced, trained musicians love and adore players with very little technique at all, and that's as it should be."

And then of course, there's (perhaps!) the modesty side of things too. He also said: "The best stuff happens when you're just sitting around playing, by miles. I don't like to sit around listening to my own records — it's perverse. I think in general that there's too much attention paid to albums just because of this business that's grown up around it. I'm going to be playing better stuff than anything on my records if I get up in a tiny bar and play with a bar band."

On balance Mark Knopfler has always advocated against the veneer of celebrity. On his approach to being famous, he said in *Sounds* in January 1983; "I really think the interest should centre around what's done rather than who is doing it. That should apply to everything, you know. I have never been madly interested in, like, what kind of socks D.H. Lawrence wore. I'm more interested in his books. But I appreciate that there's a huge gossip industry in the world and that the personality cult is definitely a happening thing, but half the time it seems to me that a lot of the people who go around appearing in the media are so busy doing *that*, they're not as interesting as the things they actually do. It's what they do that matters, not what colour sheets they've got… I think I am the same as most people. I like the things that ninety-nine percent of men like and I really feel that's one of the reasons people get into the music, because basically they feel themselves reflected in it a lot. Obviously it's a bit uncomfortable if people are pointing you out in the street all the time and I really cannot imagine how it must be for people in *Dallas* or *Coronation Street*… It's obviously obscene and ridiculous in a lot of ways and that's been said probably as long as there's been such a thing as a "celebrity". I mean, I'm prepared to take responsibility for what I do and the people who work with me and so on, but that's common to a person who runs a bakery or whatever."

Importantly, in recent years, Mark Knopfler has embraced a more balanced approach to touring and public appearances. He told *Record Collector* in May 2019; "I used to do five or six shows on the trot all the time. I've even done twenty without a day off. But at my age, you're thinking more in terms of three. It catches up with everybody. You've just got to back off the pedal a little bit, get more realistic. I'm more wary of my physical capabilities. It's manageable now; I've got better control of it so it's not spinning out of balance. Plus, I'm better at it."

And of course, his love for the guitar has never left. He said in *Guitarist* in December 2018; "A really powerful part of my childhood was gazing longingly at those things. I didn't know whether it was going to be a Futurama or a Hofner or a Burns Sonic that I was going to get first. But I was desperate for something. Boy, I loved them and I still do.

You never escape that."

John Illsley and Alan Clark performed a number of Dire Straits songs in 2009 at an open air concert in San Vigilio. Thereafter, under the band name of the Dire Straits Legends, Clark, Palmer, Illsley, Cummings, Collins, Sonni and Withers have toured as various line-ups. In a 2018 tour of the US, they were joined by Trevor Horn (of The Buggles fame) and Steve Ferrone on drums. Alan Clark released a solo piano album, *Backstory* in September 2021.

For a band named after their financial situation at the beginning of their journey, Dire Straits have come a long way. As well as being a popular band in their home country, they have made an impact with their music globally. With six studio albums and several large-scale tours behind them, they have sold more than 120 million albums worldwide and whilst a reunion doesn't seem to be on the cards, the phenomenal legacy of their music will live on.

Appendices

Band Members

Mark Knopfler: lead vocals, guitar (1977–1995)
John Illsley: bass, vocals, guitar (1977–1995)
Pick Withers: drums (1977–1982)
David Knopfler: guitar, keyboards, vocals (1977–1980)
Alan Clark: keyboards (1980–1995)
Hal Lindes: guitar (1980–1985)
Terry Williams: drums (1982–1984, 1985–1988)
Guy Fletcher: keyboards, guitar, vocals (1984–1995)
Jack Sonni: guitar (1985–1988)

Discography

Dire Straits (1978)

Side One
1. Down To The Waterline (3:55)
2. Water Of Love (5:23)
3. Setting Me Up (3:18)
4. Six Blade Knife (4:10)
5. Southbound Again (2:58)

Side Two
1. Sultans Of Swing (5:47)
2. In The Gallery (6:16)
3. Wild West End (4:42)
4. Lions (5:05)

Personnel
Dire Straits:
Mark Knopfler — vocals, lead and rhythm guitars
David Knopfler — rhythm guitar, backing vocals
John Illsley — bass guitar, backing vocals
Pick Withers — drums

Also:
Rhett Davies — engineer
Paddy Eckersley — photography
Chuck Loyola — cover painting
Bob Ludwig — remastering
Alan Schmidt — art direction
Muff Winwood — producer

Communiqué (1979)

Side One
1. Once Upon A Time In The West (5:25)
2. News (4:14)
3. Where Do You Think You're Going? (3:49)
4. Communiqué (5:49)

Side Two
1. Lady Writer (3:45)
2. Angel Of Mercy (4:36)
3. Portobello Belle (4:29)
4. Single-Handed Sailor (4:42)
5. Follow Me Home (5:50)

Personnel
Dire Straits:
Mark Knopfler — vocals, lead and rhythm guitars
David Knopfler — rhythm guitar, backing vocals
John Illsley — bass guitar, backing vocals
Pick Withers — drums

Also:
Barry Beckett (credited as B. Bear) — keyboards and producer
Geoff Halpin — illustrations
Gregg Hamm — mix engineer
Bobby Hata — mastering
Bob Ludwig — remastering
Jack Nuber — engineer
Thelbert Rigby — tape operator
Alan Schmidt — art direction
Jerry Wexler — producer
Paul Wexler — mastering supervisor

Making Movies (1980)

Side One
1. Tunnel Of Love [Extract from 'The Carousel Waltz' by Richard Rodgers and Oscar Hammerstein II] (8:11)
2. Romeo And Juliet (6:00)
3. Skateaway (6:40)

Side Two
1. Expresso Love (5:12)
2. Hand In Hand (4:48)
3. Solid Rock (3:19)
4. Les Boys (4:07)

Personnel
Dire Straits:
Mark Knopfler — vocals, guitar
John Illsley — bass guitar, vocals
Pick Withers — drums, vocals

Also:
Roy Bittan — keyboards
Sid McGinnis — guitar (uncredited)
Greg Calbi — mastering
Brian Griffin — photography
Jeff Hendrickson — assistant engineer
Jimmy Iovine — producer
Mark Knopfler — producer
Bob Ludwig — remastering
Jon Mathias — assistant engineer
Neil Terk — original design and artwork
Shelly Yakus — engineer

Love Over Gold (1982)

Side One
1. Telegraph Road (14:18)
2. Private Investigations (6:46)

Side Two
1. Industrial Disease (5:50)
2. Love Over Gold (6:17)
3. It Never Rains (7:59)

Personnel
Dire Straits:
Mark Knopfler — vocals, guitar
Hal Lindes — guitar
John Illsley — bass guitar
Alan Clark — piano, organ, synthesisers
Pick Withers — drums

Also:
Mike Mainieri — vibes, marimba (on 'Private Investigations' and 'Love Over Gold')
Ed Walsh — synthesiser programming
Barry Bongiovi — assistant engineer
Peter Cunningham — photography
Neil Dorfsman — engineer
Mark Knopfler — producer
Alan Lobel — photography
Bob Ludwig — mastering
Michael Rowe — sleeve design

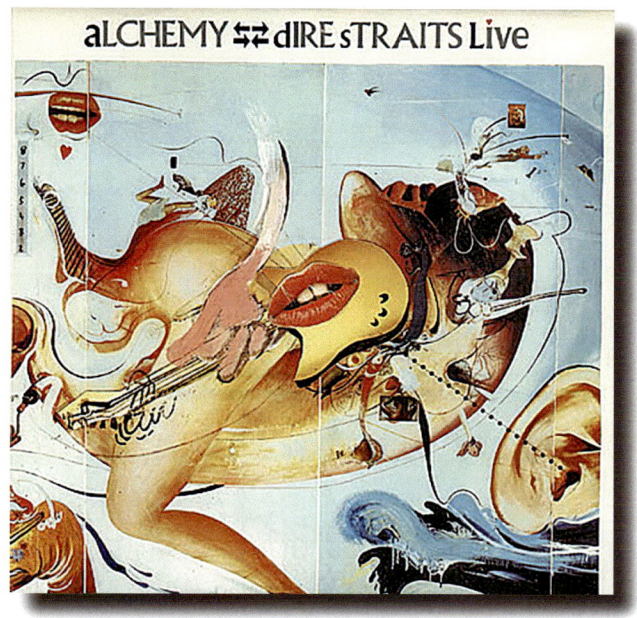

Alchemy - Dire Straits Live (1983)

Side One
1. Once Upon A Time In The West (13:01)
2. Romeo And Juliet (8:16)

Side Two
1. Expresso Love (5:36)
2. Private Investigations (7:34)
3. Sultans Of Swing (10:58)

Side Three
1. Two Young Lovers (4:52)
2. Into (The Carousel Waltz)
3. Tunnel Of Love (14:23)

Side Four
1. Telegraph Road (13:43)
2. Solid Rock (6:02)
3. Going Home - Theme From 'Local Hero' (6:02)

*The CD version also included Love Over Gold (3:28) and a slightly different running order.

Personnel:
Dire Straits:
Mark Knopfler — guitars and vocals
Hal Lindes — guitar
John Illsley — bass guitar and vocals
Alan Clark — keyboards
Guy Fletcher — keyboards and vocals
Terry Williams — drums

Also:
Tommy Mandel — Additional keyboards
Joop de Korte — percussion
Mel Collins — saxophone
Pennie Smith — photography

Brothers In Arms (1985)

Side One
1. So Far Away (3:59)
2. Money For Nothing (7:04)
3. Walk Of Life (4:12)
4. Your Latest Trick (4:46)
5. Why Worry (5:22)

Side Two
1. Ride Across The River (6:58)
2. The Man's Too Strong (4:40)
3. One World (3:40)
4. Brothers In Arms (6:59)

Personnel
Dire Straits:
Mark Knopfler — guitars and vocals
John Illsley — bass guitar and vocals
Alan Clark — keyboards
Guy Fletcher — keyboards and vocals
Omar Hakim — drums
Terry Williams — drums

Also:
Mark Knopfler, Neil Dorfsman — producers
Michael Brecker — saxophone on 'Your Latest Trick'
Randy Brecker*
Malcolm Duncan*
Neil Jason*
Tony Levin — bass on 'One World'
Jimmy Maelen*
Mike Mainieri*
Dave Plews*
Jack Sonni — guitar synthesiser on 'The Man's Too Strong'
Sting — vocals on 'Money For Nothing'
Thomas Steyer — painting
Deborah Feingold — photography
Sutton Cooper — sleeve

*Nature of contribution unspecified on album credits

On Every Street (1991)

Side One
1. Calling Elvis (6:26)
2. On Every Street (5:04)
3. When It Comes To You (5:02)
4. Fade To Black (3:49)
5. The Bug (4:18)
6. You And Your Friend (5:59)

Side Two
1. Heavy Fuel (4:57)
2. Iron Hand (3:09)
3. Ticket To Heaven (4:26)
4. My Parties (5:32)
5. Planet Of New Orleans (7:47)
6. How Long (3:53)

Personnel
Dire Straits:
Mark Knopfler — vocals, guitar
John Illsley — bass guitar
Alan Clark — organ, piano, synthesiser
Guy Fletcher — synthesisers, backing vocals

Also:
Danny Cummings — percussion
Paul Franklin — pedal steel guitar, acoustic lap steel (on 'You And Your Friend')
Vince Gill — guitar, backing vocals (on 'The Bug')
Manu Katché — percussion, drums (on 'Heavy Fuel' and 'Planet Of New Orleans')
George Martin — conductor, string arrangements (on 'Ticket To Heaven')
Phil Palmer — guitar
Jeff Porcaro — drums, percussion
Chris White — flute, saxophone
Chuck Ainlay — engineer
Mark Knopfler and Alan Clark — producers
Bob Clearmountain — mixing (on 'Heavy Fuel')
Sutton Cooper — design
Paul Cummins — design
Neil Dorfsman — mixing
Jo Motta — project coordinator
Steve Orchard — assistant engineer
Jack Joseph Puig — assistant engineer
Bill Schnee — engineer
Andy Strange — assistant engineer
Paul Williams — photography

Live Radio Albums

These records of live concerts were pressed up in small quantities for radio play and were not sold commercially but copies have found their way onto the open market.

Dire Straits / The Motors – In Concert –182
BBC Transcription Services –
CN 3179/S, 2nd October 1978

Side One
1. Down To The Waterline
2. Water Of Love
3. Wild West End
4. Sultans Of Swing
5. Lions

Side Two
5 tracks by The Motors.
Dire Straits tracks recorded live at the Paris Theatre, London, 19th July 1978.

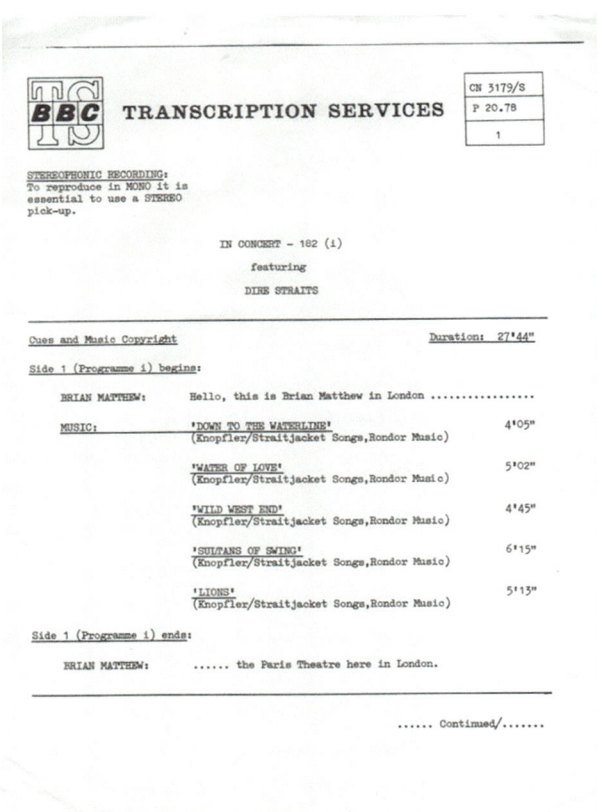

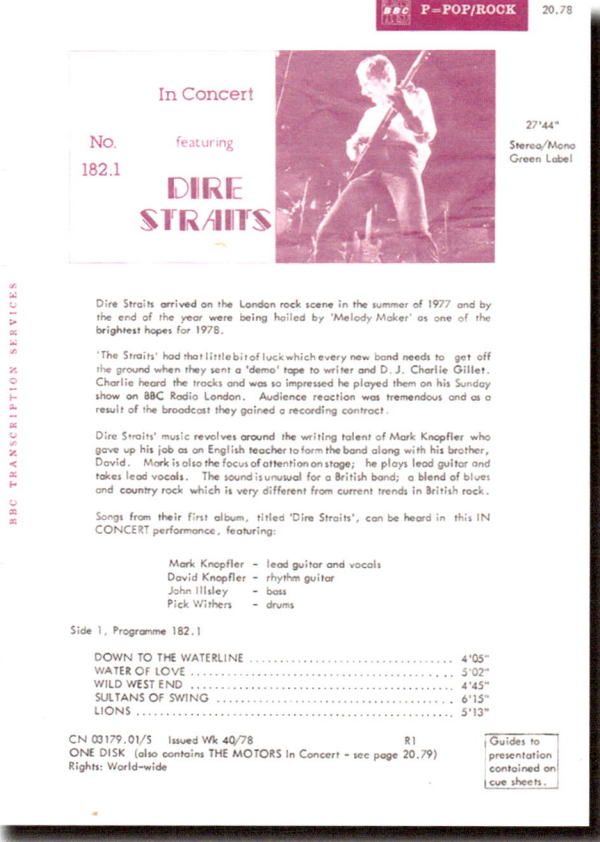

**Dire Straits – Live –
The Warner Bros. Music Show**
Warner Bros. Records – WBMS 109, 1979

Side One
1. Down To The Waterline
2. Six Blade Knife
3. In The West
4. Lady Writer
5. Where Do You Think You're Going

Side Two
1. News
2. What's The Matter
3. Lions
4. Sultans Of Swing
5. Eastbound Train
6. Southbound

Recorded at Old Waldorf, San Francisco, California, 31st March 1979.

Individual Discographies

Please note that although the following lists are extensive, they may not be exhaustive. Such has been the prolific output of everyone who made a significant contribution to Dire Straits.

Mark Knopfler

Solo Albums
Golden Heart (1996)
Sailing To Philadelphia (2000)
The Ragpicker's Dream (2002)
Shangri-La (2004)
Kill To Get Crimson (2007)
Get Lucky (2009)
Privateering (2012)
Tracker (2015)
Down The Road Wherever (2018)

Soundtracks
Local Hero (1983)
Cal (1984)
Comfort And Joy (1984)
The Princess Bride (1987)
Last Exit To Brooklyn (1989)
Wag The Dog (1997) (released in 1998)
Metroland (1999)
A Shot At Glory (2002)
Altamira (2016) with Evelyn Glennie

Collaborative Albums
Missing... Presumed Having A Good Time (1990) with The Notting Hillbillies
Neck And Neck (1990) with Chet Atkins
All The Roadrunning (2006) with Emmylou Harris
Real Live Roadrunning (2006) with Emmylou Harris

Produced Albums
Infidels - Bob Dylan (1983)
By June 1983, Dylan and Knopfler had set a preliminary sequence of nine songs, including two songs that were ultimately omitted: 'Foot Of Pride' and one of Dylan's finest songs 'Blind Willie McTell' that is just Dylan singing and playing piano with Knopfler on acoustic guitar.

Knopfler had to leave the recording sessions before the mixing stage due to Dire Straits commitments and both 'Foot Of Pride' and 'Blind Willie McTell' were dropped from consideration soon after. In later years, Knopfler claimed that "Infidels would have been a better record if I had mixed the thing, but I had to go on tour in Germany."

The two tracks were later released on The Bootleg Series Volumes 1 - 3 [Rare & Unreleased] 1961-1991 *in 1991. Knopfler also plays guitar throughout the album.*

September 2021 saw the release of Dylan's Springtime In New York: The Bootleg Series, Vol.16 (1980-1985), *a four-disc box set. Discs three and four consist of outtakes and alternative versions of tracks from the* Infidels *album produced by Knopfler and featuring his guitar work.*
Knife - Aztec Camera (1984)

Miracle - Willy DeVille (1987)
The liner notes dedicate the album to Mark and his wife "for their support which was nothing short of a Miracle in a time of Dire Straits." The final track on the album, 'Storybook Love', is the theme from The Princess Bride movie.
Land Of Dreams - Randy Newman (1988)
Knopfler produced seven of the album's twelve tracks.
The Sailor's Revenge - Bap Kennedy (2012)
Recorded at British Grove Studios in 2011.

Session Work
The Booze Brothers - Brewers Droop (1973)
Slow Train Coming - Bob Dylan (1979)
Sandy McLelland & The Backline - Sandy McLelland (1979)
Oh What A Feeling - Mavis Staples (1979)
Gaucho - Steely Dan (1980)
Solo In Soho - Phil Lynott (1980)
The Philip Lynott Album - Phil Lynott (1982)
Beautiful Vision - Van Morrison (1982)
Love Over And Over - Kate & Anna McGarrigle (1982)
Release - David Knopfler (1983)
Phil Everly - Phil Everly (1983)
Climate Of Hunter - Scott Walker (1984)
Never Told A Soul - John Illsley (1984)
The Rock Connection - Cliff Richard (1984)
Boys And Girls - Bryan Ferry (1985)
Stay Tuned - Chet Atkins (1985)
Break Every Rule - Tina Turner (1986)
The Colour Of Money Soundtrack (1986)
...Nothing Like The Sun - Sting (1987)
Primitive Dance - Paul Brady (1987)
Sails - Chet Atkins (1987)
Soldier Of Fortune - Thin Lizzy (1987)
Save The Last Dance for Me - Ben E. King (1987)
Let It Be - Ferry Aid (1987)
Prince's Trust 10th Anniversary Birthday Party (1987)
C.G.P. - Chet Atkins (1988)
Down In The Groove - Bob Dylan (1988)
Land Of Dreams - Randy Newman (1988)
Glass - John Illsley (1988)
The Shouting Stage - Joan Armatrading (1988)
Under Milk Wood (A Play For Voices) - Dylan Thomas (1988)
Foreign Affair - Tina Turner (1989)
River Of Time - The Judds (1989)
Brendan Croker & The Five O'Clock Shadows - Brendan Croker (1989)
EP - Brendan Croker & the Five O'Clock Shadows (1989)
UHF — Original Motion Picture Soundtrack And Other Stuff - Weird Al Yankovic (1989)
Hell To Pay - Jeff Healey (1990)
Knebworth: The Album (1990)
Voices That Care (1991)
The Great Indoors - Brendan Croker (1991)
Damn Right, I've Got The Blues - Buddy Guy (1991)

The Bootleg Series Volumes 1–3, 1961–1991 - Bob Dylan (1991)
Back To The Grindstone - Ronnie Milsap (1991)
Shadowdance - Chris White (1991)
Sneakin' Around - Chet Atkins (1992)
Seminole Wind - John Anderson (1992)
Country Rockers (1992)
Dulcimer Sessions - David Schnaufer (1992)
Ain't I A Woman - Rory Block (1992)
Cookin' With The Blues (1992)
Citizen Steely Dan - Steely Dan (1993)
Heartbeat - Hank Marvin (1993)
Wonderful Land (single) - Hank Marvin (1993)
Beloved One - Dee Carstensen (1993)
Don't Fall Apart On Me Tonight - Aaron Neville (1993)
Southwestern Cookin (1994)
Flyer - Nanci Griffith (1994)
Bradley Barn Sessions - George Jones (1994)
Read My Licks - Chet Atkins (1994)
Adios Amigo: A Tribute To Arthur Alexander (1994)
Confessin' The Blues (1994)
The Kershaw Sessions - Brendan Croker (1995)
Long Black Veil - The Chieftains (1995)
South Of I-10 - Sonny Landreth (1995, guest appearance)
Big River - Jimmy Nail (1995)
Just Pickin' - Steve Phillips (1996)
The Way I Should - Iris DeMent (1996)
Paradise - John Anderson (1996)
Twang!: A Tribute To Hank Marvin & The Shadows (1996)
Not Fade Away (Remembering Buddy Holly) (1996)
Throw These Guns Away + Knockin' On Heaven's Door (Dunblane tribute record) (1996)
Sult: Spirit Of The music (1996)
Pickin' The Hits - Chet Atkins (1997)
Nothin' But The Taillights - Clint Black (1997)
Blues Legends (1997)
Music For Montserrat (1997)
Closing In On The Fire - Waylon Jennings (1998)
Guilty: 30 Years of Randy Newman (1998)
Man To Woman: Men Of Note Sing For A Cause (1998)
Celtic Christmas, Vol. 4 (1998)
Tribute To Tradition (1998)
The Piper's Call - Liam O'Flynn (1998)
Austin Sessions - Kris Kristofferson (1999)
Another World - Gerry Rafferty (2000)
Showbiz Kids: The Steely Dan Story 1972–1980 (2000)
Prince's Trust 10th Anniversary Birthday Party (2000)
Buried Treasures, Vol. 3 - Lindisfarne (2000)
Guitar Heroes (2001)
Singles Collection - Hank Marvin (2001)
Timeless: Hank Williams Tribute (2001)
Good Rockin' Tonight: The Legacy Of Sun Records (2001)
Human - Rod Stewart (2001)

Jools Holland's Big Band Rhythm & Blues - Jools Holland (2002)
Chet Picks On The Grammys - Chet Atkins (2002)
RCA Country Legends - John Anderson (2002)
Vagabonds, Kings, Warriors, Angels - Thin Lizzy (2002)
Lost & Found - Lee Fardon (2002)
Parallel Tracks - the Royal Scots Dragoon Guards (2003)
Double Shot Rocks - Alan Merrill (2003)
Deja Vu (All Over Again) - John Fogerty (2004)
Is It Rolling Bob? A Reggae Tribute to Bob Dylan (2004)
Very Best Of Celtic Christmas (2004)
Guitar Ballads - Hank Marvin (2004)
Just For A Thrill - Bill Wyman's Rhythm Kings (2004)
Sea Fever - William Topley (2004)
B. B. King & Friends: 80 - B. B. King (2005, guest appearance)
Is It Rolling Bob? Dub Versions (2005)
36 Classic Guitar Favourites - Hank Marvin (2005)
Zu & Co. - The Ultimate Duets Collection - Zucchero (2005)
Prairie Home Companion Duets (2006)
East To West - Paul Burch (2006)
Take The Weather With You - Jimmy Buffett (2006)
Uncovered - Tony Joe White (2006)
Timeless (2007)
After Midnight Live - Eric Clapton (2007)
Songbird: Rare Tracks And Forgotten Gems - Emmylou Harris (2007)
The Bablake Sessions (2008)
Earth To The Dandy Warhols - The Dandy Warhols (2008, dobro)
Burning Your Playhouse Down - George Jones (2008)
From The Reach - Sonny Landreth (2008, guest appearance)
Inamorata - Guy Fletcher (2008, guest appearance)
Legacy, Vol. 1 - Jeff Healey (2009, guest appearance)
Life Goes On - Gerry Rafferty (2009)
Greatest And Latest: Just A Thrill And Live - Bill Wyman (2009)
The Secret Policeman's Balls (2009)
Live At Knebworth (2010)
Streets Of Heaven - John Illsley (2010)
Just Across The River - Jimmy Webb (2010, guest appearance)
Chet Atkins Certified Guitar Player concert-tribute to Chet Atkins (2010)
Mercury - Pieta Brown (2011)
Gathering - Diane Schuur (2011)
Freak Flag - Greg Brown (2011)
Back Pages - America (2011)
A Map Of The Floating City - Thomas Dolby (2011, guest appearance)
Memories Of My Trip - Chris Barber (2011)
's Too Much - Bo Walton (2011)
Chimes Of Freedom: Songs Of Bob Dylan (2012, guest appearance)
Impressions - Chris Botti (2012, guest appearance)
Sweet Defeat - Jon Allen (2012)
Waiting On A Dream - Bo Walton (2012)
Slightly Above Below Average - A Tribute To Chet Atkins - His Friends (2012)
Angels Without Wings - Heidi Talbot (2013)
These Wilder Things - Ruth Moody (2013)

Songs From St. Somewhere - Jimmy Buffett (2013)
The Breeze: An Appreciation Of J.J. Cale - Eric Clapton & Friends (2014)
Croz - David Crosby (2014, electric guitar on "What's Broken")
24 Karat Gold - Songs From The Vault - Stevie Nicks (2014)
Avonmore - Bryan Ferry (2014)
If This Was A Dream - Susan Ashton (2015)
The Vicar St. Sessions Vol. 1 - Paul Brady (2015)
Before This World - James Taylor (2015)
Devil Music - Randall Bramblett (2015)
Delirium - Ellie Goulding (2015)
Shadowing John Barry - Brian Bennett (2016)
Black Cat - Zucchero (2016)
Postcards - Pieta Brown (2017)
Waiting On A Song - Dan Auerbach (2017)
Have All The Songs Been Written? - The Killers (2017)
Accomplice One - Tommy Emmanuel (2018)
Freeway - Pieta Brown (2019)

David Knopfler

Solo Albums
Release (1983)
Behind The Lines (1985)
Cut The Wire (1986)
Lips Against The Steel (1988)
Lifelines (1991)
The Giver (1993)
Small Mercies (1995)
Wishbones (2001)
Ship Of Dreams (2004)
Songs For The Siren (2006)
Acoustic (with Harry Bogdanovs) (2011)
Grace (2015)
Heartlands (2019)
Last Train Leaving (2020)
Songs Of Loss And Love (2020)

John Illsley

Solo Albums
Never Told A Soul (1984)
Glass (1988)
Live In Les Baux de Provence (with Cunla and Greg Pearle) (2007)
Beautiful You (with Greg Pearle) (2008)
Streets Of Heaven (2010)
Testing The Water (2014)

Live In London (2014)
Long Shadows (2016)
Coming Up For Air (2019)

Soundtracks
Local Hero (1983)
Cal (1984)

Collaborative Albums
Private Dancer - Tina Turner (1984)

Pick Withers

Collaborative Albums
Spring - Spring (1971)
The Booze Brothers - Brewers Droop (1973)
How Long Is Forever? - Prelude (1973)
A Rare Conundrum - Bert Jansch (1977)
Slow Train Coming - Bob Dylan (1979)
Sleepwalking - Gerry Rafferty (1982)
Giant From The Blue - Gary Fletcher Band (2011)

Hal Lindes

Solo Albums
Guitar Heart (2011)
Lone Guitar (2014)
Songs For An Irish Girl (2020)

Soundtracks
Local Hero (1983)
Joyriders (1988)
Drowning In The Shallow End (1990)
Legacy — The Origins Of Civilisation (1991)
The Guilty (1992)
Born Kicking (1992)
Between The Lines (1992)
The Secrets Of Lake Success (1993)
Don't Do It (1994)
Deadly Advice (1994)
The Coriolis Effect (1994)
Bermuda Grace (1994)
Band Of Gold (1995)
The Infiltrator (1995)
Thief Takers (1995)
The Great Kandinsky (1995)

Kiss And Tell (1996)
Reckless (1997)
Gunshy (1998)
Kisses In The Dark (1998)
Big Bad World (1999)
Vent De Colère (2000)
This Is Personal (2000)
Forgive And Forget (2000)
Red Cap (2001)
Best Of Both Worlds (2001)
Local Boys (2002)
Alibi (2003)
In Denial Of Murder (2004)
Male Mail (2004)
NY-LON (2004)
Lucky 13 (2005)
Perfect Day (2005)
The Taming Of The Shrew (2005)
The Complete Guide To Parenting (2006)
Losing Gemma (2006)
Girl 27 (2007)
Little Devil (2007)
Apparitions (2008)
Off The Ledge (2009)
Albert's Memorial (2009)
The Boys Are Back (2009)
The Lucky One (2012)
A Very Secret Service (2015)

Collaborative Albums
Put It Down To Experience - Darling (1979)
Private Dancer - Tina Turner (1984)
Angel Eyes - Kiki Dee (1987)
My Way Home - Russ Taff (1989)
That's What I Like About The South - Chris Daniels & the Kings (1989)
Vigil In A Wilderness Of Mirrors - Fish (1990)
Over The Pop - Sabrina (1991)
Acoustic Connection - Clem Clempson (2000)
Midnight Blue - Twiggy (2003)
Black Coffee - Al Kooper (2005)
El Becko (Jeff Beck Tribute) (2008)
Get The Led Out (Led Zeppelin Salute) (2008)
Jimi Hendrix Tribute (Third Stone From The Sun) (2009)
Life Stories with Ian Livingstone (2009)
Irony - Sergei Vonronoff (2009)
Down To The Swamp with Robert Homes and James Homes (2015)
Acoustic Traveller with Dominik Johnson and Alex Tschallener (2017)
A Walk In The Woods with Chris Constantinou (2018)
Homebound with Chris Constantinou (2020)

Alan Clark

Solo Albums
Backstory (2021)

Soundtracks
Local Hero (1983)
The Broker's Man (1997)
Four Fathers (1999)
Most Haunted (2001)
The Inspiration (2005)

Collaborative Albums
Sleepwalking - Gerry Rafferty (1982)
Infidels - Bob Dylan (1983)
Private Dancer - Tina Turner (1984)
Empire Burlesque - Bob Dylan (1985)
Down In The Groove - Bob Dylan (1988)
North And South - Gerry Rafferty (1988)
The Shouting Stage - Joan Armatrading (1988)
Journeyman - Eric Clapton (1989)
Big River - Jimmy Nail (1995)
Crocodile Shoes II - Jimmy Nail (1996)
Life Goes On - Gerry Rafferty (2009)
Three Chord Trick (2017)
Zero Il Folle - Renato Zero (2019)
Zerosettanta - Renato Zero (2020)

Guy Fletcher

Solo Albums
Inamorata (2008)
Stone (2009)
Natural Selection (2010)
High Roads (2016)

Soundtracks
Cal (1984)
Comfort And Joy (1984)
The Princess Bride (1987)
Last Exit To Brooklyn (1989)
Wag The Dog (1997) (released in 1998)
Metroland (1999)
A Shot At Glory (2002)

Collaborative Albums
Knife - Aztec Camera (1984)
She's The Boss - Mick Jagger (1985)

Boys And Girls - Bryan Ferry (1985)
Break Every Rule - Tina Turner (1986)
Save The Last Dance For Me - Ben E. King (1987)
Land Of Dreams - Randy Newman (1988)
Missing… Presumed Having A Good Time - Notting Hillbillies (1990)
Neck And Neck - Mark Knopfler and Chet Atkins (1990)
Mamouna - Bryan Ferry (1994)
Golden Heart - Mark Knopfler (1996)
Siren - Heather Nova (1998)
Sailing To Philadelphia - Mark Knopfler (2000)
The Ragpicker's Dream - Mark Knopfler (2002)
Shangri-La - Mark Knopfler (2004)
All The Roadrunning - Mark Knopfler and Emmylou Harris (2006)
Kill To Get Crimson - Mark Knopfler (2007)
Get Lucky - Mark Knopfler (2009)
Privateering - Mark Knopfler (2012)
Tracker - Mark Knopfler (2015)
Down The Road Wherever - Mark Knopfler (2018)

Produced Albums
Belouis Some - Belouis Some (1986). Fletcher co-produced with Gary Langan.
Get Lucky - Mark Knopfler (2009). Fletcher co-produced with Mark Knopfler.

Terry Williams

Soundtracks
Local Hero (1983)
Cal (1984)
Comfort And Joy (1984)

Collaborative Albums
To Live For To Die - Man (1970)
Man - Man (1971)
Do You Like It Here Now, Are You Settling In? - Man (1971)
Rockpile - Rockpile (1972)
Greasy Truckers Party - Man (1972)
Be Good To Yourself At Least Once A Day - Man (1972)
Back Into The Future - Man (1973)
Iceberg - Deke Leonard (1973)
Kamikaze - Deke Leonard (1974)
Rhinos, Winos, And Lunatics - Man (1974)
Slow Motion - Man (1974)
Maximum Darkness - Man (1975)
The Welsh Connection - Man (1976)
All's Well That Ends Well - Man (1977)
Get It - Rockpile (1977)
Juppanese - Mickey Jupp (1978)
Carlene Carter - Carlene Carter (1978)

Tracks On Wax 4 - Rockpile (1978)
Jesus Of Cool (Pure Pop For Now People in US) - Nick Lowe (1978)
Labour Of Lust - Nick Lowe (1979)
Repeat When Necessary - Rockpile (1979)
Seconds Of Pleasure - Rockpile (1980)
Musical Shapes - Carlene Carter (1980)
Tenement Steps - The Motors (1980)
Twangin... - Rockpile (1981)
Before Your Very Eyes - Deke Leonard (1981)
Nick The Knife - Nick Lowe (1982)
C'est C Bon - Carlene Carter (1983)
Phil Everly - The Everly Brothers (1983)
EB 84 - The Everly Brothers (1984)
Rock Connection - Cliff Richard (1984)
Bash! - Billy Bremner (1984)
Never Told A Soul - John Illsley (1984)
Private Dancer - Tina Turner (1984)
You Caught Me Out - Tracey Ullman (1984)
Willie And The Poor Boys - Willie And The Poor Boys (1985)
Full Moon - Paul Brady (1986)
Pinker And Prouder Than Previous - Nick Lowe (1988)
The Mona Lisa's Sister - Graham Parker (1988)
Yo Frankie - Dion (1989)
Undrugged - Man (2002) (1996 sessions)

Awards

Honoured and Inducted
PRS for Music Heritage Award 2009
Rock and Roll Hall of Fame 2018

Won
Brit Awards 1980 — British Group
Brit Awards 1986 — British Group
Grammy Award 1986 — Best Rock Performance by a Duo Or Group (for 'Money For Nothing')
Grammy Award 1986 — Best Engineered Recording, Non-Classical (for *Brothers In Arms*, Mark Knopfler Neil Dorfsman engineer)
Juno Award 1986 — International Album of the Year
MTV Video Music Award 1986 — Video of the Year (for 'Money For Nothing')
MTV Video Music Award 1986 — Best Group Video (for 'Money For Nothing')
Brit Awards 1987 — British Album of the Year (for *Brothers In Arms*)
Grammy Award 1987 — Best Music Video (for 'Brothers In Arms')
Grammy Award 2006 — Best Surround Sound Album (for his surround sound production for *Brothers In Arms* — 20th Anniversary Edition, Chuck Ainlay, surround mix engineer; Bob Ludwig, surround mastering engineer; Chuck Ainlay and Mark Knopfler, surround producers)

Nominated
Grammy Award 1980 — Best New Artist
Grammy Award 1980 — Best Rock Vocal Performance by a Duo or Group (for 'Sultans Of Swing')
American Music Award 1986 — Favourite Pop/Rock Single (for 'Money For Nothing')
Brit Awards 1986 — British Album of the Year (for *Brothers In Arms*)
Brit Awards 1986 — British Single (for 'Money For Nothing')
Brit Awards 1986 — British Video (for 'Money For Nothing')
Grammy Award 1986 — Album of the Year (for *Brothers In Arms*)

Grammy Award 1986 — Record of the Year (for 'Money For Nothing')
Grammy Award 1986 — Song of the Year (for 'Money For Nothing')
MTV Video Music Award 1986 — Best Concept Video (for 'Money For Nothing')
MTV Video Music Award 1986 — Most Experimental Video (for 'Money For Nothing')
MTV Video Music Award 1986 — Best Stage Performance in a Video (for 'Money For Nothing')
MTV Video Music Award 1986 — Best Overall Performance in a Video (for 'Money For Nothing')
MTV Video Music Award 1986 — Best Direction in a Video (for 'Money For Nothing')
MTV Video Music Award 1986 — Best Visual Effects in a Video (for 'Money For Nothing')
MTV Video Music Award 1986 — Best Art Direction in a Video (for 'Money For Nothing')
MTV Video Music Award 1986 — Best Editing in a Video (for 'Money For Nothing')
MTV Video Music Award 1986 — Viewer's Choice (for 'Money For Nothing')
Brit Awards 1987 — British Group
Brit Awards 1992 — British Group
Grammy Award 1992 — Best Music Video (for 'Calling Elvis')
Brit Awards 2010 — British Album of Thirty Years (for *Brothers In Arms*)

Tour Dates

1977

Sunday 26th June	Farrer House, Crossfields, Deptford, London, England
Thursday 28th July	Albany Empire, Deptford, London, England
Tuesday 2nd August	Tramshed, Woolwich, London, England
Sunday 4th September	Hope & Anchor, Islington, London, England
Saturday 10th September	Albany Empire, Deptford, London England (evening gig)
Monday 11th September	Clapham Common Bandstand, London, England (afternoon gig)
Monday 11th September	Hope & Anchor, Islington, London, England (evening gig)
Wednesday 13th September	Broadway Queen Deptford London England
Sunday 18th September	Hope & Anchor, Islington, London, England
Thursday 22nd September	Hope & Anchor, Islington, London, England
Sunday 25th September	Hope & Anchor, Islington, London, England
Wednesday 12th October	Rock Garden, Covent Garden, London, England
Saturday 15th October	Dingwalls, Chalk Farm, London, England
Thursday 20th October	Rock Garden, Covent Garden, London, England
Friday 28th October	Bedford Hill, London, England
Tuesday 1st November	Dingwalls, Chalk Farm, London, England
Wednesday 2nd November	Rock Garden, Covent Garden, London, England
Friday 4th November	Hope & Anchor, Islington, London, England
Tuesday 8th November	Rock Garden Covent Garden London England
Friday 11th November	Hope & Anchor, Islington, London, England
Saturday 12th November	Leveller, London, England
Wednesday 16th November	Rock Garden, Covent Garden, London, England
Friday 18th November	Hope & Anchor, Islington, London, England
Friday 25th November	Hope & Anchor, Islington, London, England
Monday 28th November	Rock Garden, Covent Garden, London, England
Friday 9th December	Front Row Festival, Hope & Anchor, Islington, London, England
Tuesday 13th December	Dingwalls, Chalk Farm, London, England
Thursday 15th December	Rock Garden, Covent Garden, London, England

Saturday 17th December	Champers Wine Bar, London, England
Monday 19th December	Loughton College, Essex, England
Wednesday 21st December	Dingwalls, Chalk Farm, London, England
unknown date	Broadway Queen Club, Deptford, London, England

1978

Tuesday 10th January	Dingwalls, Chalk Farm, London, England
Friday 13th January	Rock Garden, Covent Garden, London, England
Tuesday 17th January	Nashville Rooms, Kensington, London, England
Friday 20th January	University, Sheffield, England
Saturday 21st January	University, Manchester, England
Sunday 22nd January	Eric's, Liverpool, England
Monday 23rd January	Outlook Club, Doncaster, England
Tuesday 24th January	Friars, Aylesbury, England
Wednesday 25th January	University, Southampton, England
Thursday 26th January	University, Leicester, England
Friday 27th January	Polytechnic, Newcastle, England
Saturday 28th January	Polytechnic, Huddersfield, England
Sunday 29th January	Roundhouse, Chalk Farm, London, England
Monday 30th January	Polytechnic, Leeds, England
Wednesday 1st February	Top Rank, Brighton, England
Thursday 2nd February	Barbarella's, Birmingham, England
Friday 3rd February	Civic Hall, St. Albans, England
Saturday 4th February	Oasis, Swindon, England
Sunday 5th February	Greyhound, Croydon, England
Tuesday 14th March	Marquee Club, London, England
Saturday 18th March	Paris Theatre, London, England (BBC Recording)
Sunday 19th March	Chester College, England
Tuesday 21st March	Marquee Club, London, England
Tuesday 28th March	Marquee Club, London, England
Saturday 1st April	Hope & Anchor, Islington, London, England
Wednesday 5th April	Honky Tonk, Wimbledon, London, England
Monday 10th April	Arts Centre, Poole, England
Tuesday 11th April	Marquee Club, London, England
Wednesday 19th April	Quaintway's Club, Chester, England
Wednesday 3rd May	Lyceum, London, England
Thursday 4th May	Hippodrome, Birmingham, England
Friday 5th May	University, Lancaster, England
Saturday 6th May	Queen Margaret Union, Glasgow, Scotland
Sunday 7th May	Apollo Theatre, Manchester, England
Monday 8th May	City Hall, Sheffield, England
Tuesday 9th May	Top Rank, Cardiff, Wales
Wednesday 10th May	Castaways, Plymouth, England
Thursday 11th May	Arts Centre, Poole, England
Friday 12th May	Town Hall, Torquay, England
Saturday 13th May	Polytechnic, Leicester, England
Friday 14th May	Hippodrome, Bristol, England
Thursday 18th May	Albany Empire, Deptford, London, England

First overseas dates as support to Styx:

Monday 22nd May	Theatre Mogador, Paris, France
Tuesday 23rd May	Congresgebouw, Den Haag, The Netherlands
Wednesday 24th May	Musikhalle, Hamburg, West Germany
Thursday 25th May	Neue Welt, Berlin, West Germany
Sunday 28th May	Circus Krone, Munich, West Germany
Monday 29th May	Erlangen Stadthalle, Nuremberg, West Germany
Tuesday 30th May	Stadthalle, Offenbach, West Germany
Wednesday 31st May	Rhein-Neckar Halle, Heidelberg, West Germany
Thursday 1st June	Volkshaus, Zurich, Switzerland

All the above shows in grey were cancelled due to a member of Styx taking ill.

Monday 5th June	Odeon Theatre, Edinburgh, Scotland
Friday 9th June	Lafayette, Wolverhampton, England
Saturday 10th June	JB's, Dudley, England
Tuesday 13th June	University, Sheffield, England
Wednesday 14th June	Polytechnic, Huddersfield, England
Thursday 15th June	University, Leicester, England
Friday 16th June	Country Club, Kirklevington, England
Saturday 17th June	Rock Garden, Middlesbrough, England
Sunday 18th June	Forde Green Hotel, Leeds, England
Tuesday 20th June	Tiffany's, Edinburgh, Scotland
Wednesday 21st June	Technical College, Dundee, Scotland
Friday 23rd June	76 Club, Burton-on-Trent, England
Saturday 24th June	Boat Hall, Nottingham, England
Sunday 25th June	Memorial Hall, Newbridge, England
Tuesday 27th June	Rafters, Manchester, England
Wednesday 28th June	Talk Of The East, Lowestoft, England
Thursday 29th June	Granary, Bristol, England
Friday 30th June	Metro Club, Plymouth, England
Saturday 1st July	Polytechnic, Oxford, England
Sunday 2nd July	Albany, Deptford London England
Tuesday 4th July	Barbarella's, Birmingham, England
Wednesday 5th July	Marquee Club, London, England
Thursday 6th July	Marquee Club, London, England
Friday 8th July	Civic Hall, St. Albans, England
Saturday 9th July	ATV, Birmingham, England
Wednesday 19th July	Paris Theatre, London, England (BBC Recording)
Wednesday 11th October	Zaal Lux, Herenthout, Belgium
Thursday 12th October	Stadschouwburg, Mechelen, Belgium
Friday 13th October	Casino, Berengen, Belgium
Saturday 14th October	Empire, Paris, France
Sunday 15th October	Grone Maarsen, Zedelgen, Belgium
Monday 16th October	University, Leuven, Belgium
Wednesday 18th October	Huize Maas, Groningen, Netherlands
Thursday 19th October	Stadschouwburg, Rotterdam, Netherlands
Friday 20th October	Stadschouwburg, Eindhoven, Netherlands
Saturday 21st October	Vereeniging, Nijmegen, Netherlands
Sunday 22nd October	Stadschouwburg, Sittart, Netherlands
Monday 23rd October	Paradiso, Amsterdam, Netherlands
Wednesday 25th October	Bursschouwburg, Brussels, Belgium
Saturday 28th October	Musikhalle, Hamburg, West Germany
Sunday 29th October	Neue Welt, Berlin, West Germany
Wednesday 1st November	University, Bradford, England
Thursday 2nd November	Polytechnic, Nottingham, England
Friday 3rd November	Polytechnic, Newcastle, England
Saturday 4th November	University, Durham, England
Sunday 5th November	Civic Hall, Dunstable, England
Wednesday 8th November	University, Keele, England
Thursday 9th November	University, Hull, England
Friday 10th November	University, York, England
Saturday 11th November	University, Sheffield, England
Monday 13th November	Town Hall, Birmingham, England

Tuesday 14th November	University, Leicester, England
Wednesday 15th November	University, Manchester, England
Thursday 16th November	Polytechnic, Leeds, England
Friday 17th November	Polytechnic, Bristol, England
Saturday 18th November	College Of Education, Hitchin, England

1979

Sunday 11th February	De Doelen, Rotterdam, Netherlands
Monday 12th February	Niedersachsenhalle, Hanover, West Germany
Tuesday 13th February	Philipshalle, Düsseldorf, West Germany
Wednesday 14th February	Rosengarten, Mannheim, West Germany
Thursday 15th February	Stadthalle Stolberg West Germany
Friday 16th February	Rockpalast WDR (TV), Cologne, West Germany
Sunday 18th February	Stadthalle, Bremen, West Germany
Friday 23rd February	Paradise, Boston, USA
Saturday 24th February	Paradise, Boston, USA
Sunday 25th February	Alumni, Providence, USA
Monday 26th February	Shaboo, Williamantic, USA
Wednesday 28th February	Hullabaloo, Albany, USA
Friday 2nd March	Bottom Line, New York, USA
Saturday 3rd March	Bottom Line, New York, USA
Tuesday 6th March	Tower Theatre, Philadelphia, USA
Thursday 8th March	Bayou, Washington, USA
Friday 9th March	Bayou, Washington, USA
Sunday 11th March	After Dark, Buffalo, USA
Monday 12th March	Agora, Cleveland, USA
Tuesday 13th March	University, Toronto, Canada
Wednesday 14th March	Plateau Auditorium, Montreal, Canada
Thursday 15th March	Centrestage, Detroit, USA
Friday 16th March	Park West, Chicago, USA
Saturday 17th March	Palms, Milwaukee, USA
Monday 19th March	Memorial Hall, Kansas, USA
Wednesday 21st March	Opry House, Houston, USA
Thursday 22nd March	Opry House,, Austin USA
Friday 23rd March	Palladium, Dallas, USA
Sunday 25th March	Regis College, Denver, USA
Tuesday 27th March	Roxy, San Diego, USA
Wednesday 28th March	Roxy, Los Angeles, USA
Thursday 29th March	Roxy, Los Angeles, USA
Saturday 31st March	Old Waldorf, San Francisco, USA
Sunday 1st April	Old Waldorf, San Francisco, USA
Monday 2nd April	University Of Davis, Sacramento, USA
Wednesday 23rd May	Stadthalle, Offenbach, West Germany
Thursday 24th May	Stadthalle, Offenbach, West Germany
Friday 25th May	Sporthalle, Stuttgart, West Germany
Saturday 26th May	Küernackhalle, Würzburg, West Germany
Sunday 27th May	Stadthalle, Wettingen, Switzerland

Tuesday 29th May	Circus Krone, Munich, West Germany
Wednesday 30th May	Hemmerleinhalle, Nuremberg, West Germany
Thursday 31st May	Rhein-Neckar-Halle, Heidelberg, West Germany
Friday 1st June	Circus Krone, Munich, West Germany
Saturday 2nd June	Stadthalle, Freiberg, West Germany
Monday 4th June	Pinkpop Festival, Sportpark, Geleen, Netherlands
Tuesday 5th June	Palais Des Sports, Paris, France
Friday 8th June	Empire, Liverpool, England
Saturday 9th June	Apollo, Glasgow, Scotland
Sunday 10th June	Odeon, Edinburgh, Scotland
Monday 11th June	City Hall, Sheffield, England
Wednesday 13th June	Odeon, Birmingham, England
Thursday 14th June	City Hall, Newcastle, England
Friday 15th June	Apollo, Manchester, England
Saturday 16th June	Colston Hall, Bristol, England
Sunday 17th June	Hammersmith Odeon, London, England
Monday 18th June	Dome, Brighton, England
Wednesday 20th June	Hammersmith Odeon, London, England
Thursday 21st June	Hammersmith Odeon, London, England
Saturday 23rd June	Loreley Festival, Frankfurt, West Germany
Sunday 24th June	Westfalenhalle (Festival), Dortmund, West Germany
Friday 29th June	Deutschlandhalle (Festival), Berlin, West Germany
Sunday 1st July	Olympiastadion (Festival), Munich, West Germany
Saturday 7th July	Festival, Torhout, Belgium
Sunday 8th July	Werchter Festival, Brussels, Belgium
Saturday 8th September	Orpheum, Boston, USA
Sunday 9th September	Ocean State Theatre, Providence, USA
Monday 10th September	Calderone Theatre, Hampstead, USA
Tuesday 11th September	Palladium, New York, USA
Thursday 13th September	Capitol Theatre, Passaic, USA
Friday 14th September	Tower Theatre, Philadelphia, USA
Saturday 15th September	Smith Centre, Washington, USA
Monday 17th September	Chrysler Hall, Norfolk, USA
Tuesday 18th September	Coliseum, Greensboro, USA
Thursday 20th September	Park Centre, Charlotte, USA
Friday 21st September	Fox Theatre, Atlanta, USA
Sunday 23rd September	Civic Auditorium, Jacksonville, USA
Monday 24th September	Curtis Hixon, Tampa, USA
Tuesday 25th September	Jai Alai, Miami, USA
Friday 28th September	Township, Columbia, USA
Saturday 29th September	Coliseum, Knoxville, USA
Monday 1st October	Gardens, Louisville, USA
Tuesday 2nd October	Bogarts, Cincinnati, USA
Wednesday 3rd October	Palace Theatre, Cleveland, USA
Thursday 4th October	Centrestage, Detroit, USA
Saturday 6th October	Kiel Opera House, St. Louis, USA
Sunday 7th October	Uptown Theatre, Chicago, USA
Thursday 1st November	Ahoy, Rotterdam, Netherlands
Friday 2nd November	Vereeniging, Nijmegen, Netherlands
Saturday 3rd November	Vereeniging, Nijmegen, Netherlands
Sunday 4th November	Carre Theatre, Amsterdam, Netherlands

Monday 5th November	Carre Theatre, Amsterdam, Netherlands
Wednesday 7th November	Ijsselhal, Zwolle, Netherlands
Thursday 8th November	Grugahalle, Essen, West Germany
Friday 9th November	Messehalle, Cologne, West Germany
Sunday 11th November	Münsterlandhalle, Münster, West Germany
Monday 12th November	Stadthalle, Braunschweig, West Germany
Tuesday 13th November	CCH, Hamburg, West Germany
Wednesday 14th November	Ostseehalle, Kiel, West Germany
Friday 16th November	Idraettenshus, Vejle, Denmark
Saturday 17th November	Olympen, Lund, Sweden
Sunday 18th November	Tivoli Theatre, Copenhagen, Denmark
Monday 19th November	Tivoli Theatre, Copenhagen, Denmark
Tuesday 20th November	Scandinavium, Gothenburg, Sweden
Wednesday 21st November	Ekeberghalle, Oslo, Norway
Friday 23rd November	Johanneshov, Stockholm, Sweden
Monday 26th November	Weser-Ems-Halle, Oldenburg, West Germany
Thursday 27th November	Forêt Nationale, Brussels, Belgium
Tuesday 11th December	Stadium, Dublin, Ireland
Wednesday 12th December	Stadium, Dublin, Ireland
Thursday 13th December	Whitla Hall, Belfast, Northern Ireland
Friday 14th December	Whitla Hall, Belfast, Northern Ireland
Tuesday 18th December	Lewisham Odeon, London, England
Wednesday 19th December	Lewisham Odeon, London, England
Thursday 20th December	Rainbow Theatre, London, England
Friday 21st December	Rainbow Theatre, London, England

1980

Wednesday 22nd October	Commodore, Vancouver, Canada
Thursday 23rd October	Showbox, Seattle, USA
Friday 24th October	State University, Portland, USA
Sunday 26th October	Old Waldorf, San Francisco, USA
Monday 27th October	Old Waldorf, San Francisco, USA
Tuesday 28th October	Roxy, Los Angeles, USA
Wednesday 29th October	Roxy, Los Angeles, USA
Friday 31st October	*Fridays* (TV), Los Angeles, USA
Sunday 2nd November	Agora, Dallas, USA
Monday 3rd November	Armadillo, Austin, USA
Tuesday 4th November	Agora, Houston, USA
Wednesday 5th November	Saenger Performing Arts Centre, New Orleans, USA
Thursday 6th November	State University, Baton Rouge, USA
Friday 7th November	Brothers Music Hall, Birmingham, USA
Saturday 8th November	Agora, Atlanta, USA
Sunday 9th November	Exit Inn, Nashville, USA
Tuesday 11th November	Bayou, Washington, USA
Wednesday 12th November	Emerald City, Philadelphia, USA
Thursday 13th November	Stage West, Hartford, USA
Friday 14th November	Bea Theatre, New York, USA

Saturday 15th November	Capitol Theatre, Passaic, USA
Sunday 16th November	Berklee Performance Centre, Boston, USA
Tuesday 18th November	Agora, Cleveland, USA
Wednesday 19th November	Royal Oak, Detroit, USA
Thursday 20th November	Park West, Chicago, USA
Friday 21st November	Park West, Chicago, USA
Sunday 23rd November	Massey Hall, Toronto, Canada
Wednesday 26th November	*Top Of The Pops* (TV) London England
Saturday 29th November	*Old Grey Whistle Test* (TV) London England
Monday 1st December	Victoria Hall, Hanley, England
Tuesday 2nd December	Apollo, Manchester, England
Wednesday 3rd December	Apollo, Manchester, England
Thursday 4th December	City Hall, Sheffield, England
Friday 5th December	City Hall, Sheffield, England
Saturday 6th December	Apollo, Glasgow, Scotland
Sunday 7th December	Capitol, Aberdeen, Scotland
Monday 8th December	Playhouse, Edinburgh, Scotland
Tuesday 9th December	City Hall, Newcastle, England
Wednesday 10th December	City Hall, Newcastle, England
Friday 12th December	University, Lancaster, England
Saturday 13th December	The Refectory, Leeds, England
Sunday 14th December	Odeon, Birmingham, England
Sunday 15th December	Odeon, Birmingham, England
Monday 16th December	Assembly Rooms, Derby, England
Tuesday 17th December	Gaumont, Ipswich, England
Wednesday 18th December	Gaumont, Southampton, England
Thursday 19th December	Westfalenhalle, Dortmund, West Germany
Friday 20th December	Westfalenhalle, Dortmund, West Germany
Monday 22nd December	Rainbow Theatre, London, England
Tuesday 23rd December	Rainbow Theatre, London, England
Wednesday 24th December	Rainbow Theatre, London, England
Wednesday 31st December	Stadium, Dublin, Ireland

1981

Thursday 1st January	Stadium, Dublin, Ireland
Friday 2nd January	City Hall, Cork, Ireland
Saturday 3rd January	Leisureland, Galway, Ireland
Monday 5th January	Ulster Hall, Belfast, Northern Ireland
Tuesday 6th January	Ulster Hall, Belfast, Northern Ireland
Thursday 5th February	Teatro Ariston, Sanremo, Italy (Sanremo Music Festival)
Friday 6th February	Teatro Ariston, Sanremo, Italy (Sanremo Music Festival)
Sunday 22nd March	Entertainment Centre, Perth, Australia
Wednesday 25th March	Festival Hall, Melbourne, Australia
Thursday 26th March	Festival Hall, Melbourne, Australia
Friday 27th March	Festival Hall, Melbourne, Australia
Saturday 28th March	Festival Hall, Melbourne, Australia
Sunday 29th March	Festival Hall, Melbourne, Australia
Monday 30th March	Festival Theatre, Adelaide, Australia
Tuesday 31st March	Festival Theatre, Adelaide, Australia
Wednesday 1st April	Festival Theatre, Adelaide, Australia
Thursday 2nd April	Festival Theatre, Adelaide, Australia
Saturday 4th April	Regent Theatre, Sydney, Australia
Sunday 5th April	Regent Theatre, Sydney, Australia
Monday 6th April	Regent Theatre, Sydney, Australia
Tuesday 7th April	Regent Theatre, Sydney, Australia
Wednesday 8th April	Regent Theatre, Sydney, Australia
Thursday 9th April	Regent Theatre, Sydney, Australia
Friday 10th April	Festival Hall, Brisbane, Australia
Saturday 11th April	Festival Hall, Brisbane, Australia
Wednesday 15th April	Western Springs, Auckland, New Zealand
Tuesday 5th May	Rhein-Main-Halle, Wiesbaden, West Germany
Wednesday 6th May	Rhein-Main-Halle, Wiesbaden, West Germany
Thursday 7th May	Rhein-Neckar-Halle, Heidelberg, West Germany
Friday 8th May	Freiheitshalle, Hof, West Germany
Saturday 9th May	Hemmerleinhalle, Nuremberg, West Germany
Tuesday 12th May	Olympiahalle, Munich, West Germany
Wednesday 13th May	Messehalle, Stuttgart, West Germany
Thursday 14th May	Sporthalle, Cologne, West Germany
Friday 15th May	Philipshalle, Düsseldorf, West Germany
Saturday 16th May	Grugahalle, Essen, West Germany
Monday 18th May	Eissporthalle, Kassel, West Germany
Tuesday 19th May	Niedersachsenhalle, Hanover, West Germany
Wednesday 20th May	Eissporthalle, Berlin, West Germany
Thursday 21st May	CCH, Hamburg, West Germany
Friday 22nd May	CCH, Hamburg, West Germany
Sunday 24th May	Randershalle, Randers, Denmark
Monday 25th May	Forum, Copenhagen, Denmark
Tuesday 26th May	Gröna Lund, Stockholm Sweden
Thursday 28th May	Drammenhalle, Oslo, Norway
Friday 29th May	Scandinavium Gothenburg Sweden
Sunday 31st May	UKK Halli, Helsinki, Finland
Monday 1st June	UKK Halli, Helsinki, Finland
Saturday 13th June	Rodahal, Kerkrade, Netherlands

Sunday 14th June	Jaap Edenhal, Amsterdam, Netherlands
Monday 15th June	De Doelen, Rotterdam, Netherlands
Tuesday 16th June	Rijnhal, Arnhem, Netherlands
Thursday 18th June	Palais Des Sports, Paris, France
Saturday 20th June	Hallenstadion, Zurich, Switzerland
Sunday 21st June	Patinoir Des Vernets, Geneva, Switzerland
Tuesday 23rd June	Palais Des Sports, Bordeaux, France
Thursday 25th June	Palais Des Sports, Lyon, France
Friday 26th June	Antique Theatre, Orange, France
Saturday 27th June	Stadio Comunale, San Remo, Italy
Sunday 28th June	Stadio Comunale, Carrara, Italy
Monday 29th June	Vigorelli, Milan, Italy
Tuesday 30th June	Antistadio, Bolonga, Italy
Wednesday 1st July	Stadio Comunale, Turin, Italy
Saturday 4th July	Festival, Torhout, Belgium
Sunday 5th July	Werchter Festival, Brussels, Belgium
Monday 6th July	Centre Sportif, Differdange, Luxembourg

1982

Tuesday 30th November	Civic Hall, Guildford, England
Wednesday 1st December	City Hall, Sheffield, England
Thursday 2nd December	City Hall, Sheffield, England
Friday 3rd December	Spa Royal Hall, Bridlington, England
Saturday 4th December	Leisure Centre, Deeside, England
Sunday 5th December	Apollo, Glasgow, Scotland
Monday 6th December	Playhouse, Edinburgh, Scotland
Tuesday 7th December	Playhouse, Edinburgh, Scotland
Wednesday 8th December	City Hall, Newcastle, England
Thursday 9th December	City Hall, Newcastle, England
Friday 10th December	Apollo, Manchester, England
Saturday 11th December	Apollo, Manchester, England
Sunday 12th December	Gaumont, Ipswich, England
Monday 13th December	De Montfort Hall, Leicester, England
Tuesday 14th December	National Exhibition Centre, Birmingham, England
Wednesday 15th December	The Centre, Brighton, England
Thursday 16th December	The Centre, Brighton, England
Friday 17th December	National Exhibition Centre, Birmingham, England
Saturday 18th December	Wembley Arena, London, England
Sunday 19th December	Wembley Arena, London, England
Monday 20th December	Wembley Arena, London, England
Tuesday 21st December	Wembley Arena, London, England

1983

Friday 4th March	Hordern Pavilion, Sydney, Australia
Saturday 5th March	Hordern Pavilion, Sydney, Australia
Sunday 6th March	Hordern Pavilion, Sydney, Australia
Monday 7th March	Hordern Pavilion, Sydney, Australia
Tuesday 8th March	Hordern Pavilion, Sydney, Australia
Wednesday 9th March	Hordern Pavilion, Sydney, Australia
Friday 11th March	Festival Hall, Brisbane, Australia
Saturday 12th March	Festival Hall, Brisbane, Australia
Sunday 13th March	Festival Hall, Brisbane, Australia
Tuesday 15th March	Indoor Sports Centre, Canberra, Australia
Thursday 17th March	Memorial Drive Tennis Stadium, Adelaide, Australia
Friday 18th March	Memorial Drive Tennis Stadium, Adelaide, Australia
Saturday 19th March	Festival Hall, Melbourne, Australia
Sunday 20th March	Festival Hall, Melbourne, Australia
Monday 21st March	Festival Hall, Melbourne, Australia
Tuesday 22nd March	Festival Hall, Melbourne, Australia
Thursday 24th March	Entertainment Centre, Perth, Australia
Saturday 26th March	Western Springs, Auckland, New Zealand
Tuesday 29th March	Athletic Park, Wellington, New Zealand
Saturday 2nd April	Seinenken Hall, Tokyo, Japan
Sunday 3rd April	Seinenken Hall, Tokyo, Japan

Monday 4th April	Seinenken Hall, Tokyo, Japan
Tuesday 5th April	Expo Hall, Osaka, Japan
Wednesday 11th May	Ernst Merck-Halle, Hamburg, West Germany
Thursday 12th May	Brøndby Hallen, Copenhagen, Denmark
Saturday 14th May	Deutschlandhalle, Berlin, West Germany
Sunday 15th May	Eissporthalle, Kassel, West Germany
Monday 16th May	Sporthalle, Cologne, West Germany
Wednesday 18th May	Stadthalle, Vienna, Austria
Thursday 19th May	Stadhalle, Linz, Austria
Friday 20th May	Olympiahalle, Munich, West Germany
Saturday 21st May	Festhalle, Frankfurt, West Germany
Sunday 22nd May	Ebert-Halle, Ludwigshafen, West Germany
Monday 23rd May	Hallenstadion, Zürich, Switzerland
Tuesday 24th May	Hallenstadion, Zürich, Switzerland
Wednesday 25th May	Patinoir Des Vernets, Geneva, Switzerland
Thursday 26th May	Patinoir Des Vernets, Geneva, Switzerland
Friday 27th May	Palais Des Sports, Grenoble, France
Saturday 28th May	St. Jakob Sporthalle, Basel, Switzerland
Sunday 29th May	Renhus, Strasbourg, France
Monday 30th May	Centre Sportif, Petange, Luxembourg
Tuesday 31st May	Forêt Nationale, Brussels, Belgium
Wednesday 1st June	Forêt Nationale, Brussels, Belgium
Sunday 12th June	Ijsselhal, Zwolle, Netherlands
Monday 13th June	Maasport, Den Bosch, Netherlands
Tuesday 14th June	Jaap Edenhal, Amsterdam, Netherlands
Thursday 16th June	Ahoy, Rotterdam, Netherlands
Friday 17th June	Rodahal, Kerkrade, Netherlands
Saturday 18th June	Parc Des Expositions, Lille, France
Sunday 19th June	Palais Des Sports, Paris, France
Monday 20th June	Palais Des Sports, Paris, France
Tuesday 21st June	Palais Des Sports, Paris, France
Wednesday 22nd June	Palais Des Sports, Paris, France
Thursday 23rd June	Palais Des Sports, Paris, France
Friday 24th June	La Beaujoire, Nantes, France
Sunday 26th June	Les Arènes, Bayonne, France
Tuesday 28th June	Estadio Roman Valero, Madrid, Spain
Thursday 30th June	Levante Futbol Estadio, Valencia, Spain
Friday 1st July	Estadio Municipal Narcis Sala, Barcelona, Spain
Sunday 3rd July	Arènes, Beziers, France
Tuesday 5th July	Stadio Comunale, Novara, Italy
Wednesday 6th July	Stadio Comunale, Ferrara, Italy
Thursday 7th July	Stadio Comunale, Prato (Florence), Italy
Friday 8th July	Le Capannelle, Rome, Italy
Saturday 9th July	Stadio Comunale, Cava Dei Tirenni (Naples), Italy
Tuesday 12th July	Maksimir Stadium, Zagreb, Yugoslavia
Sunday 17th July	Punchestown Racecourse, Naas, Ireland
Wednesday 20th July	Dominion Theatre, London, England
Friday 22nd July	Hammersmith Odeon, London, England
Saturday 23rd July	Hammersmith Odeon, London, England

1985

Thursday 25th April	Sportski Centar Gripe, Split, Yugoslavia
Tuesday 30th April	Sultanpool, Jerusalem, Israel
Wednesday 1st May	City Park, Tel Aviv, Israel
Thursday 2nd May	City Park, Tel Aviv, Israel
Monday 6th May	Sportspalace, Athens, Greece
Tuesday 7th May	Sportspalace, Athens, Greece
Wednesday 8th May	Golden Rose Festival, Montreux, Switzerland
Thursday 9th May	Golden Rose Festival, Montreux, Switzerland
Friday 10th May	Hala Pionir, Belgrade, Yugoslavia
Saturday 11th May	Hala Pionir, Belgrade, Yugoslavia
Sunday 12th May	Dom Sportova, Zagreb, Yugoslavia
Monday 13th May	Tivoli, Ljubljana, Yugoslavia
Tuesday 14th May	Eishalle, Graz, Austria
Wednesday 15th May	Stadthalle, Vienna, Austria
Thursday 16th May	Sportshall, Budapest, Hungary
Friday 17th May	Sportshall, Budapest, Hungary
Saturday 18th May	Sportshall, Budapest, Hungary
Sunday 19th May	Sportshall, Budapest, Hungary
Wednesday 22nd May	P.O.C., Eindhoven, Netherlands
Thursday 23rd May	Rijnhal, Arnhem, Netherlands
Friday 24th May	Jaap Edenhal, Amsterdam, Netherlands
Saturday 25th May	Ahoy, Rotterdam, Netherlands
Sunday 26th May	Limburghal, Genk, Belgium
Monday 27th May	Forêt Nationale, Brussels, Belgium
Tuesday 28th May	Palais Des Sports, Caen, France
Wednesday 29th May	Parc De Penfeld, Brest, France
Thursday 30th May	La Beaujoire, Nantes, France
Friday 31st May	Patinoire, Bordeaux, France
Saturday 1st June	Plaza De Toros Vista Alegre, Bilbao, Spain
Monday 3rd June	Estadio Roman Valero, Madrid, Spain
Wednesday 5th June	Municipal Velodrome, Barcelona, Spain
Thursday 6th June	Municipal Velodrome, Barcelona, Spain
Friday 7th June	Palais Des Sports, Toulouse, France
Saturday 8th June	Palais Des Sports, Toulouse, France
Monday 10th June	Stade Louis II, Monaco
Tuesday 11th June	Arènes Orange, Monaco
Wednesday 12th June	Palais Des Sports, Grenoble, France
Thursday 13th June	Patinoire, Geneva, Switzerland
Friday 14th June	Patinoire, Geneva, Switzerland
Saturday 15th June	Patinoire, Geneva, Switzerland
Sunday 16th June	Hallenstadion, Zürich, Switzerland
Monday 17th June	Hallenstadion, Zürich, Switzerland
Tuesday 18th June	St. Jakob Sporthalle, Basel, Switzerland
Wednesday 19th June	St. Jakob Sporthalle, Basel, Switzerland
Thursday 20th June	Palais Des Sports, Dijon, France
Friday 21st June	Patinoire De Kockelscheuer, Luxembourg, Luxembourg
Saturday 22nd June	Brielpoort, Deinze, Belgium
Sunday 23rd June	Palais Omnisports De Bercy, Paris, France
Monday 24th June	Palais Omnisports De Bercy, Paris, France

Tuesday 25th June	Palais Omnisports De Bercy, Paris, France
Friday 28th June	National Exhibition Centre, Birmingham, England
Saturday 29th June	National Exhibition Centre, Birmingham, England
Sunday 30th June	National Exhibition Centre, Birmingham, England
Monday 1st July	National Exhibition Centre, Birmingham, England
Tuesday 2nd July	Conference Centre, Brighton, England
Wednesday 3rd July	Conference Centre, Brighton, England
Thursday 4th July	Wembley Arena, London, England
Friday 5th July	Wembley Arena, London, England
Saturday 6th July	Wembley Arena, London, England
Sunday 7th July	Wembley Arena, London, England
Monday 8th July	Wembley Arena, London, England
Tuesday 9th July	Wembley Arena, London, England
Wednesday 10th July	Wembley Arena, London, England
Thursday 11th July	Wembley Arena, London, England
Friday 12th July	Wembley Arena, London, England
Saturday 13th July	Live Aid, Wembley Stadium, London, England
Sunday 14th July	Wembley Arena, London, England
Monday 15th July	Wembley Arena, London, England
Tuesday 16th July	Wembley Arena, London, England
Tuesday 23rd July	Forum, Montreal, Canada
Wednesday 24th July	Civic Centre, Ottawa, Canada
Thursday 25th July	Civic Centre, Ottawa, Canada
Friday 26th July	Varsity Arena, Toronto, Canada
Saturday 27th July	Varsity Arena, Toronto, Canada
Sunday 28th July	Varsity Arena, Toronto, Canada
Monday 29th July	Varsity Arena, Toronto, Canada
Thursday 1st August	Roy Wilken's Auditorium, St. Paul, USA
Friday 2nd August	Auditorium, Milwaukee, USA
Saturday 3rd August	Poplar Creek, Chicago, USA
Sunday 4th August	Pine Knob, Detroit, USA
Monday 5th August	Blossom Music Centre, Cleveland, USA
Tuesday 6th August	Syria Mosque, Pittsburgh, USA
Wednesday 7th August	Mann Music Centre, Philadelphia, USA
Thursday 8th August	Merriweather Post Pavilion Washington USA
Saturday 10th August	Fox Theatre, Atlanta, USA
Sunday 11th August	ennessee Performing Arts Centre, Nashville, USA
Tuesday 13th August	Zoo Amphitheatre, Oklahoma City, USA
Wednesday 14th August	Reunion Arena, Dallas, USA
Thursday 15th August	Coliseum, Austin, USA
Friday 16th August	Majestic Theatre, San Antonio, USA
Saturday 17th August	Summit Theatre, Houston, USA
Tuesday 3rd September	Red Rocks Amphitheatre, Denver, USA
Wednesday 4th September	Red Rocks Amphitheatre, Denver, USA
Friday 6th September	Activity Centre, Tempe, USA
Saturday 7th September	State University, Dan Diego, USA
Sunday 8th September	Pacific Amphitheatre, Costa Mesa, USA
Monday 9th September	Greek Theatre, Los Angeles, USA
Tuesday 10th September	Greek Theatre, Los Angeles, USA
Wednesday 11th September	Greek Theatre, Los Angeles, USA
Thursday 12th September	Greek Theatre, Los Angeles, USA

Friday 13th September	Concord Pavilion, San Francisco, USA
Saturday 14th September	Concord Pavilion, San Francisco, USA
Sunday 15th September	Memorial Auditorium, Sacramento, USA
Tuesday 17th September	Civic Auditorium, Portland, USA
Wednesday 18th September	Civic Auditorium, Portland, USA
Thursday 19th September	Arena, Seattle, USA
Friday 20th September	Arena, Seattle, USA
Saturday 21st September	UBC Gym, Vancouver, Canada
Sunday 22nd September	Arena, Victoria, USA
Monday 23rd September	P.N.E., Vancouver, Canada
Tuesday 24th September	Coliseum, Edmonton, Canada
Wednesday 25th September	Saddledome, Calgary, Canada
Thursday 26th September	Coliseum, Edmonton, Canada
Friday 27th September	Saddledome, Calgary, Canada
Tuesday 1st October	Radio City Music Hall, New York, USA
Wednesday 2nd October	Radio City Music Hall, New York, USA
Thursday 3rd October	Radio City Music Hall, New York, USA
Friday 4th October	Civic Centre, Providence, USA
Saturday 5th October	Wang Centre, Boston, USA
Sunday 6th October	Wang Centre, Boston, USA
Monday 7th October	Cumberland County Civic Centre, Portland, USA
Tuesday 8th October	Boston Gardens, Boston, USA
Wedensday 9th October	Civic Centre, Hartford, USA
Thursday 10th October	Civic Centre, Hartford, USA
Friday 11th October	Nassau Coliseum, Uniondale, New York, USA
Saturday 12th October	Madison Square Garden, New York, USA
Tuesday 22nd October	Drammenhalle, Oslo, Norway
Wednesday 23rd October	Drammenhalle, Oslo, Norway
Thursday 24th October	Café Opera, Stockholm, Sweden
Friday 25th October	Johanneshov, Stockholm, Sweden
Satuday 26th October	Johanneshov, Stockholm, Sweden
Monday 28th October	Ice Hall, Helsinki, Finland
Tuesday 29th October	Ice Hall, Helsinki, Finland
Thursday 31st October	Brøndby Hallen, Copenhagen, Denmark
Friday 1st November	Brøndby Hallen, Copenhagen, Denmark
Saturday 2nd November	Alsterdorfer Sporthalle, Hamburg, West Germany
Sunday 3rd November	Martinihal, Groningen, Netherlands
Thursday 4th November	Eilenreidhalle, Hannover, West Germany
Friday 5th November	Deutschlandhalle, Berlin, West Germany
Thursday 7th November	Stadthalle, Vienna, Austria
Friday 8th November	Basketball-Halle, Munich, West Germany
Saturday 9th November	Eishalle, Wels, Austria
Sunday 10th November	Eishalle, Graz, Austria
Monday 11th November	Sporthalle, Linz, Austria
Tuesday 12th November	Olympic Hall, Innsbruck, Austria
Thursday 14th November	Parc Des Expositions, Lyon, France
Friday 15th November	Maison Des Sports, Clermont-Ferrand, France
Monday 18th November	Frankenhalle, Nuremberg, West Germany
Tuesday 19th November	Hanns-Martin-Schleyer-Halle, Stuttgart, West Germany
Wednesday 20th November	Festhalle, Frankfurt, West Germany
Thursday 21st November	Sporthalle, Cologne, West Germany

Friday 22nd November	Grugahalle, Essen, West Germany
Saturday 23rd November	Groenoordhal, Leiden, Netherlands
Sunday 24th November	Groenoordhal, Leiden, Netherlands
Monday 25th November	Forêt Nationale, Brussels, Belgium
Wednesday 27th November	alais Omnisports De Bercy, Paris, France
Thursday 28th November	Palais Omnisports De Bercy, Paris, France
Friday 29th November	Palais Omnisports De Bercy, Paris, France
Saturday 30th November	Palais Omnisports De Bercy, Paris, France
Tuesday 3rd December	City Hall, Newcastle, England
Wednesday 4th December	City Hall, Newcastle, England
Thursday 5th December	City Hall, Newcastle, England
Friday 6th December	City Hall, Newcastle, England
Saturday 7th December	Apollo, Manchester, England
Sunday 8th December	Apollo, Manchester, England
Monday 9th December	Apollo, Manchester, England
Tuesday 10th December	Apollo, Manchester, England
Wednesday 11th December	Leisure Centre, Deeside, England
Thursday 12th December	Leisure Centre, Deeside, England
Friday 13th December	Showering Pavilion, Shepton Mallett, England
Saturday 14th December	Showering Pavilion, Shepton Mallett, England
Sunday 15th December	National Exhibition Centre, Birmingham, England
Monday 16th December	National Exhibition Centre, Birmingham, England
Tuesday 17th December	Hammersmith Odeon, London, England
Wednesday 18th December	Hammersmith Odeon, London, England
Thursday 19th December	Hammersmith Odeon, London, England
Friday 20th December	Hammersmith Odeon, London, England
Saturday 21st December	Hammersmith Odeon, London, England
Sunday 22nd December	Hammersmith Odeon, London, England
Monday 23rd December	Hammersmith Odeon, London, England
Sunday 29th December	Playhouse, Edinburgh, Scotland
Monday 30th December	Playhouse, Edinburgh, Scotland
Tuesday 31st December	Playhouse, Edinburgh, Scotland

1986

Friday 7th February	King George V Oval, Hobart, Australia
Saturday 8th February	King George V Oval, Hobart, Australia
Wednesday 12th February	Westlake Stadium, Adelaide, Australia
Friday 14th February	Sports And Entertainment Centre, Melbourne, Australia
Saturday 15th February	Sports And Entertainment Centre, Melbourne, Australia
Sunday 16th February	Sports And Entertainment Centre, Melbourne, Australia
Monday 17th February	Sports And Entertainment Centre, Melbourne, Australia
Tuesday 18th February	Sports And Entertainment Centre, Melbourne, Australia
Wednesday 19th February	Sports And Entertainment Centre, Melbourne, Australia
Thursday 20th February	Sports And Entertainment Centre, Melbourne, Australia
Friday 21st February	Sports And Entertainment Centre, Melbourne, Australia
Saturday 22nd February	Sports And Entertainment Centre, Melbourne, Australia
Sunday 23rd February	Sports And Entertainment Centre, Melbourne, Australia
Monday 24th February	Myer Music Bowl, Melbourne, Australia
Tuesday 25th February	Myer Music Bowl, Melbourne, Australia
Wednesday 26th February	Olympic Park Oval No. 1, Melbourne, Australia
Saturday 1st March	Mount Smart Stadium, Auckland, New Zealand
Sunday 2nd March	Western Springs, Auckland, New Zealand
Tuesday 4th March	Athletic Park, Wellington, New Zealand
Friday 7th March	Addington Showgrounds, Christchurch, New Zealand
Monday 10th March	Entertainment Centre, Sydney, Australia
Tuesday 11th March	Entertainment Centre, Sydney, Australia
Wednesday 12th March	Entertainment Centre, Sydney, Australia
Thursday 13th March	Entertainment Centre, Sydney, Australia
Friday 14th March	Entertainment Centre, Sydney, Australia
Saturday 15th March	Entertainment Centre, Sydney, Australia
Sunday 16th March	Entertainment Centre, Sydney, Australia
Monday 17th March	Entertainment Centre, Sydney, Australia
Tuesday 18th March	Entertainment Centre, Sydney, Australia
Wednesday 19th March	Entertainment Centre, Sydney, Australia
Thursday 20th March	Entertainment Centre, Sydney, Australia
Friday 21st March	Entertainment Centre, Sydney, Australia
Saturday 22nd March	Entertainment Centre, Sydney, Australia
Sunday 23rd March	Sydney Cricket Ground, Sydney, Australia
Monday 24th March	Entertainment Centre, Sydney, Australia
Tuesday 25th March	Boondall Sports And Entertainment Centre, Brisbane, Australia
Wednesday 26th March	Boondall Sports And Entertainment Centre, Brisbane, Australia
Thursday 27th March	Boondall Sports And Entertainment Centre, Brisbane, Australia
Saturday 29th March	Sound Shell, Rockhampton, Australia
Monday 31st March	Showgrounds, Mackay, Australia
Wednesday 2nd April	Dean Park, Townsville, Australia
Friday 4th April	Showgrounds, Cairns, Australia
Tuesday 8th April	Showgrounds, Darwin, Australia
Friday 11th April	Ayers Rock, Australia
Sunday 13th April	Entertainment Centre, Perth, Australia
Monday 14th April	Entertainment Centre, Perth, Australia
Tuesday 15th April	Entertainment Centre, Perth, Australia
Wednesday 16th April	Entertainment Centre, Perth, Australia
Thursday 17th April	Entertainment Centre, Perth, Australia

Friday 18th April	Entertainment Centre, Perth, Australia
Saturday 19th April	Entertainment Centre, Perth, Australia
Sunday 20th April	Entertainment Centre, Perth, Australia
Wednesday 23rd April	Entertainment Centre, Sydney, Australia
Thursday 24th April	Entertainment Centre, Sydney, Australia
Friday 25th April	Entertainment Centre, Sydney, Australia
Saturday 26th April	Entertainment Centre, Sydney, Australia

1988

Monday 6th June	Prince's Trust Rock Gala, Royal Albert Hall, London, England
Wednesday 8th June	Hammersmith Odeon, London, England
Thursday 9th June	Hammersmith Odeon, London, England
Saturday 11th June	Mandela 70th Birthday Tribute concert, Wembley Stadium, London, England

1989

Monday 9th October	Mayfair, Newcastle, England (Charity concert)

1990

Monday 30th June	Knebworth Festival, Hertfordshire, England

1991

Friday 23rd August	Point Depot, Dublin, Ireland
Saturday 24th August	Point Depot, Dublin, Ireland
Sunday 25th August	Point Depot, Dublin, Ireland
Monday 26th August	Point Depot, Dublin, Ireland
Tuesday 27th August	Point Depot, Dublin, Ireland
Friday 30th August	Sheffield Arena, Sheffield, England
Saturday 31st August	Sheffield Arena, Sheffield, England
Sunday 1st September	Sheffield Arena, Sheffield, England
Monday 2nd September	Sheffield Arena, Sheffield, England
Tuesday 3rd September	Sheffield Arena, Sheffield, England
Thursday 5th September	National Exhibition Centre, Birmingham, England
Friday 6th September	National Exhibition Centre, Birmingham, England
Saturday 7th September	National Exhibition Centre, Birmingham, England
Sunday 8th September	National Exhibition Centre, Birmingham, England
Monday 9th September	National Exhibition Centre, Birmingham, England
Wednesday 11th September	Scottish Exhibition And Conference Centre, Glasgow, Scotland
Thursday 12th September	cottish Exhibition And Conference Centre, Glasgow, Scotland
Friday 13th September	Scottish Exhibition And Conference Centre, Glasgow, Scotland
Saturday 14th September	cottish Exhibition And Conference Centre, Glasgow, Scotland

Monday 16th September	Wembley Arena, London, England
Tuesday 17th September	Wembley Arena, London, England
Wednesday 18th September	Wembley Arena, London, England
Thursday 19th September	Wembley Arena, London, England
Friday 20th September	Wembley Arena, London, England
Monday 23rd September	Westfalenhalle, Dortmund, Germany
Tuesday 24th September	Westfalenhalle, Dortmund, Germany
Wednesday 25th September	Westfalenhalle, Dortmund, Germany
Thursday 26th September	tadthalle, Bremen, Germany
Friday 27th September	Stadthalle, Bremen, Germany
Saturday 28th September	Ahoy, Rotterdam, Netherlands
Sunday 29th September	Ahoy, Rotterdam, Netherlands
Monday 30th September	Ahoy, Rotterdam, Netherlands
Tuesday 1st October	Forest National, Brussels, Belgium
Wednesday 2nd October	Forest National, Brussels, Belgium
Thursday 3rd October	Palais Omnisports De Bercy, Paris, France
Friday 4th October	Palais Omnisports De Bercy, Paris, France
Saturday 5th October	Palais Omnisports De Bercy, Paris, France
Monday 7th October	Festhalle, Frankfurt, Germany
Tuesday 8th October	Festhalle, Frankfurt, Germany
Wednesday 9th October	Festhalle, Frankfurt, Germany
Friday 11th October	Olympiahalle, Munich, Germany
Saturday 12th October	Olympiahalle, Munich, Germany
Monday 14th October	Hallenstadion, Zürich, Switzerland
Tuesday 29th October	Entertainment Centre, Sydney, Australia
Wednesday 30th October	Entertainment Centre, Sydney, Australia
Thursday 31st October	Entertainment Centre, Sydney, Australia
Friday 1st November	Entertainment Centre, Sydney, Australia
Saturday 2nd November	Entertainment Centre, Sydney, Australia
Sunday 3rd November	Entertainment Centre, Sydney, Australia
Monday 4th November	Entertainment Centre, Sydney, Australia
Tuesday 5th November	Entertainment Centre, Sydney, Australia
Thursday 7th November	Entertainment Centre, Brisbane, Australia
Friday 8th November	Entertainment Centre, Brisbane, Australia
Saturday 9th November	Entertainment Centre, Brisbane, Australia
Sunday 10th November	Entertainment Centre, Brisbane, Australia
Monday 11th November	Entertainment Centre, Brisbane, Australia
Wednesday 13th November	Flinders Park National Tennis Centre, Melbourne, Australia
Thursday 14th November	Flinders Park National Tennis Centre, Melbourne, Australia
Friday 15th November	Flinders Park National Tennis Centre, Melbourne, Australia
Saturday 16th November	Flinders Park National Tennis Centre, Melbourne, Australia
Sunday 17th November	Flinders Park National Tennis Centre, Melbourne, Australia
Monday 18th November	Flinders Park National Tennis Centre, Melbourne, Australia
Saturday 14th December	Lancaster Park, Christchurch, New Zealand
Friday 20th December	Athletic Park, Wellington, Australia
Saturday 21st December	Athletic Park, Wellington, Australia

1992

Thursday 30th January	Arco Arena, Sacramento, USA
Friday 31st January	Lawlor Events Centre, Reno, USA
Saturday 1st February	Oakland Coliseum, San Francisco, USA
Sunday 2nd February	Oakland Coliseum, San Francisco, USA
Tuesday 4th February	Selland Coliseum, Fresno, USA
Wednesday 5th February	Sports Arena, San Diego, USA
Thursday 6th February	Bally's, Las Vegas, USA
Friday 7th February	Great Western Forum, Los Angeles, USA
Saturday 8th February	Great Western Forum, Los Angeles, USA
Monday 10th February	Veterans Memorial Coliseum, Phoenix, USA
Thursday 13th February	Summit, Houston, USA
Friday 14th February	Reunion Arena, Dallas, USA
Sunday 16th February	Kemper Arena, Kansas City, USA
Monday 17th February	Illinois University, Champaign, USA
Tuesday 18th February	Rosemont Horizon, Chicago, USA
Wednesday 19th February	Palace Of Auburn Hills, Detroit, USA
Thursday 20th February	Richfield Coliseum, Cleveland, USA
Friday 21st February	University, Dayton, USA
Sunday 23rd February	Meadowlands Arena, East Rutherford, USA
Monday 24th February	Capital Centre, Largo, USA
Tuesday 25th February	Broome County Arena, Binghamton, USA
Wednesday 26th February	Madison Square Garden, New York, USA
Friday 28th February	Nassau Coliseum, Uniondale, New York, USA
Saturday 29th February	Knickerbocker Arena, Albany, USA
Sunday 1st March	Civic Centre, Providence, USA
Monday 2nd March	Spectrum, Philadelphi,a USA
Tuesday 3rd March	Spectrum, Philadelphia, USA
Wednesday 4th March	War Memorial, Syracuse, USA
Thursday 5th March	Centrum, Worcester, USA
Friday 6th March	Civic Centre, Hartford, USA
Monday 9th March	Metro Centre, Halifax, USA
Tuesday 10th March	Metro Centre, Halifax, USA
Wednesday 11th March	Coliseum Moncton, New Brunswick, Canada
Thursday 12th March	Colisee, Québec, Canada
Friday 13th March	Forum, Montreal, Canada
Saturday 14th March	Civic Arena, Ottawa, Canada
Monday 16th March	Civic Arena, Ottawa, Canada
Tuesday 17th March	Copps Coliseum, Hamilton, Canada
Thursday 19th March	Maple Leaf Gardens, Toronto, Canada
Friday 20th March	Maple Leaf Gardens, Toronto, Canada
Saturday 21st March	Arena, Sudbury, Canada
Tuesday 24th March	Arena, Winnipeg, Canada
Thursday 26th March	Agridome, Regina, Canada
Friday 27th March	Saskatchewan Place, Saskatoon, Canada
Saturday 28th March	Northlands Coliseum, Edmonton, Canada
Sunday 29th March	Saddledome, Calgary, Canada
Monday 30th March	Olympic Saddledome, Calgary, Canada
Tuesday 31st March	P.N.E., Vancouver, Canada
Wednesday 1st April	P.N.E., Vancouver, Canada

Friday 3rd April	Spokane, Coliseum, Washington, USA
Saturday 4th April	Coliseum, Seattle, USA
Monday 6th April	Memorial Coliseum, Portland, USA
Saturday 18th April	Galaxy, Metz, France
Sunday 19th April	Galaxy, Metz, France
Monday 20th April	Halle Tony Garnier, Lyon, France
Tuesday 21st April	Halle Tony Garnier, Lyon, France
Wednesday 22nd April	Palais Des Sports, Grenoble, France
Friday 24th April	Palais Omnisports De Bercy, Paris, France
Saturday 25th April	Palais Omnisports De Bercy, Paris, France
Sunday 26th April	Palais Omnisports De Bercy, Paris, France
Monday 27th April	Palais Omnisports De Bercy, Paris, France
Tuesday 28th April	Palais Omnisports De Bercy, Paris, France
Wednesday 29th April	Palais Omnisports De Bercy, Paris, France
Thursday 30th April	Palais Omnisports De Bercy, Paris, France
Saturday 2nd May	Parc De Penfold, Brest, France
Monday 4th May	La Patinoire, Bordeaux, France
Tuesday 5th May	Velódrome de Anoeta, San Sebastian, Spain
Wednesday 6th May	Velódrome de Anoeta, San Sebastian, Spain
Friday 8th May	Plaza De Toros Monumental, Barcelona, Spain
Saturday 9th May	Plaza De Toros Monumental, Barcelona, Spain
Sunday 10th May	Plaza De Toros Monumental, Barcelona, Spain
Wednesday 13th May	Estadio Vicente Calderón, Madrid, Spain
Saturday 16th May	Estadio de Alvalade, Lisbon, Portugal
Tuesday 19th May	Les Arènes, Nîmes, France
Wednesday 20th May	Les Arènes, Nîmes, France
Thursday 21st May	Les Arènes, Nîmes, France
Sunday 24th May	Stade De La Beaujore, Nantes, France
Wednesday 27th May	Werchter Festival Site, Brussels, Belgium
Friday 29th May	Feyenoord Stadium, Rotterdam, Netherlands
Saturday 30th May	Feyenoord Stadium, Rotterdam, Netherlands
Sunday 31st May	Feyenoord Stadium, Rotterdam, Netherlands
Monday 1st June	Feyenoord Stadium, Rotterdam, Netherlands
Wednesday 3rd June	Earls Court, London, England
Friday 4th June	Earls Court, London, England
Saturday 5th June	Earls Court, London, England
Sunday 6th June	Earls Court, London, England
Monday 7th June	Earls Court, London, England
Tuesday 8th June	Earls Court, London, England
Thursday 11th June	Cardiff Arms Park, Cardiff, Wales
Saturday 13th June	International Stadium, Gateshead, England
Tuesday 16th June	Maine Road, Manchester, England
Thursday 18th June	Portman Road, Ipswich, England
Saturday 20th June	Woburn Abbey, Woburn, England
Thursday 25th June	La Pontaise, Lausanne, Switzerland
Saturday 27th June	Fussballstadion St. Jakob, Basel, Switzerland
Sunday 28th June	Fussballstadion St. Jakob, Basel, Switzerland
Tuesday 30th June	Hanns-Martin-Schleyer-Halle, Stuttgart, Germany
Friday 3rd July	Praterstadion, Vienna, Austria
Sunday 5th July	Fussballstadion, Linz, Austria
Tuesday 7th July	Waldstadion, Frankfurt, Germany

Thursday 9th July	Wildparkstadion, Karlsruhe, Germany
Saturday 11th July	Olympiastadion, Munich, Germany
Monday 13th July	Zeppelinfeld, Nuremberg, Germany
Wednesday 15th July	Alsterdorfer Sporthalle, Hamburg, Germany
Thursday 16th July	Alsterdorfer Sporthalle, Hamburg, Germany
Friday 17th July	Mungersdorfer Stadion, Cologne, Germany
Saturday 18th July	Mungersdorfer Stadion, Cologne, Germany
Monday 20th July	Waldbühne Amphitheatre, Berlin, Germany
Tuesday 21st July	Waldbühne Amphitheatre, Berlin, Germany
Wednesday 22nd July	Waldbühne Amphitheatre, Berlin, Germany
Saturday 25th July	Weserstadion, Bremen, Germany
Monday 27th July	Gentofte Stadium, Copenhagen, Denmark
Tuesday 28th July	Gentofte Stadium, Copenhagen, Denmark
Thursday 30th July	Vallehovin Stadium, Oslo, Norway
Friday 31st July	Café Opera, Stockholm, Sweden
Saturday 1st August	Olympic Stadium, Stockholm, Sweden
Tuesday 4th August	Olympic Stadium, Helsinki, Finland
Friday 7th August	Ice Stadium, Gothenborg, Denmark
Saturday 8th August	Ice Stadium, Gothenborg, Denmark
Thursday 20th August	Estadio Municipal de Balaidos, Vigo, Spain
Saturday 22nd August	Estadio del Molinón, Gijón, Spain
Tuesday 25th August	Estadio Sao Luis, Faro, Portugal
Thursday 27th August	Campo de Fútbol Municipal, Marbella, Spain
Saturday 29th August	Campo de Fútbol Principe Felipe, Cáceres, Spain
Monday 31st August	Plaza De Toros, Pamplona, Spain
Tuesday 1st September	Plaza De Toros Vista Alegre, Bilbao, Spain
Thursday 3rd September	Parc Lescure, Bordeaux, France
Saturday 5th September	Stade De L'Ouest, Nice, France
Monday 7th September	Forum Di Assago, Milan, Italy
Tuesday 8th September	Forum Di Assago, Milan, Italy
Wednesday 9th September	Forum Di Assago, Milan, Italy
Thursday 10th September	Forum Di Assago, Milan, Italy
Friday 11th September	Arena, Verona, Italy
Saturday 12th September	Arena, Verona, Italy
Monday 14th September	Stadio Del Baseball, Florence, Italy
Wednesday 16th September	Paleur, Rome, Italy
Thursday 17th September	Paleur, Rome, Italy
Saturday 19th September	Stadio Comunale Cava Dei, Tirenni, Italy
Tuesday 22nd September	Halle Tony Garnier, Lyon, France
Wednesday 23rd September	Halle Tony Garnier, Lyon, France
Friday 25th September	Stade De Sapiac, Montauban (Toulouse), France
Saturday 26th September	Stade De Sapiac, Montauban (Toulouse), France
Monday 28th September	Les Arènes, Nîmes, France
Tuesday 29th September	Les Arènes, Nîmes, France
Wednesday 30th September	Les Arènes, Nîmes, France
Friday 2nd October	Palau Sant Jordi, Barcelona, Spain
Saturday 3rd October	Palau Sant Jordi, Barcelona, Spain
Sunday 4th October	Palau Sant Jordi, Barcelona, Spain
Tuesday 6th October	Plaza de Toros de Las Ventas, Madrid, Spain
Wednesday 7th October	Plaza de Toros de Las Ventas, Madrid, Spain
Friday 9th October	Estadio de la Romareda, Zaragoza, Spain